For the Hard Ones:
A Lesbian Phenomenology
Para las duras: Una fenomenología lesbiana

For the Hard Ones:
A Lesbian Phenomenology
Para las duras: Una fenomenología lesbiana

tatiana de la tierra

sapphic classics from
A MIDSUMMER NIGHT'S PRESS
& SINISTER WISDOM

A Midsummer Nights Press
amidsummernightspress@gmail.com
www.amidsummernightspress.com

Sinister Wisdom, Inc.
2333 McIntosh Road
Dover, FL 33527
sinisterwisdom@gmail.com
www.sinisterwisdom.org

Designed by Nieves Guerra

Cover: Photograph by Hilary Cellini Cook. Editing to image by Kim Meyerer. Courtesy of the tatiana de la tierra private collection.

First edition, April 2018

ISBN-13: 978-1-938334-34-4

Cataloging-in-Publication data provided by the author and by literary executors

de la tierra, tatiana, 1961-2012
        For the hard ones: a lesbian phenomenology = Para las duras: una fenomenología lesbiana / tatiana de la tierra. (First edition – San Diego, CA: Calaca Press and Buffalo, NY: Chibcha Press; 2002) Revised edition – Dover, FL: Sinister Wisdom; 2018.
        144 p. ; cm

        Text in English and Spanish (side by side translations)
        Includes bibliographical references (p. 137-139)
        ISBN: 978-1-938334-34-4

Suggested Library of Congress subject headings:
        1. Lesbianism – Philosophy – Poetry. 2. Lesbians – Identity. 3. Lesbian erotica. 4. Coming out (sexual orientation) I. Title. II. Title : Para las duras.

Printed in the U.S. on recycled paper.

descendieron prendidas la una de la otra. parecía una cadena de acero rutilante, brilloso con el sol que era de mediodía y de verano. parecían bucaneras al asalto.
vorágines, cristales, vientos
abrasadores azogue, parecían
armaduras y espadas de cristal. la cadena bajaba de la nave como guirnalda de violetas y acacias y anémonas y rosas y lirios de los valles cruzando el aire gráciles como hojitas de bosques en otoño. como gitanas, descendían. como filibusteras sin batallas ni gritos de victoria.

Albalucía Angel, *Las andariegas*

Photo of original *For the Hard Ones* cover: Original cover and book design by tatiana de la tierra and Kim Meyerer. Cover painting "Smoking Prayer" © 2002 by Maya Gonzalez, www.mayagonzalez.com

they descended holding onto one another. it resembled a chain of shining steel, glittering in the midday summer sun. they seemed like buccaneers ready to strike, maelstroms, crystals, harsh winds

of quicksilver, they seemed

armor and swords of crystal. the chain came down from the ship like a garland of violets and acacias and anemones and roses and lilies of the valley crossing the air, slender like tiny autumn leaves. like gypsy women, they descended. like pirates without battles or cries of victory.

Albalucía Angel, *The Wanderers*

Photo of original *For the Hard Ones* cover: Original cover and book design by tatiana de la tierra and Kim Meyerer. Cover painting "Smoking Prayer" © 2002 by Maya Gonzalez, www.mayagonzalez.com

Contenido / Contents

Foreword

I had the lesbian pleasure of being bullied by tatiana de la tierra.

This happened at a queer archive at the University of California, Los Angeles. I was celebrating the release of my first book, and I trembled at the podium while I read to a small audience about Chicana goths dyking out in the 90s.

I had never met tatiana and did not know what she looked like. I knew of her but didn't realize it was she who sat in the front row, staring at me. She wore a tie-dye t-shirt, a goddess necklace, and a facial expression that lacked amusement. Her stare made me feel targeted. Its gaze was unapologetic, impolite, and tightly pointed. These qualities concerned me. They also titillated me.

tatiana occupied a significant amount of space, she spilled off her folding chair and into the air, but it was her body language that communicated intent. Before me sat a stranger with premeditated purpose.

When my reading concluded, tatiana sprang from her chair. She bypassed my friends and acquaintances and made a beeline that brought us face to face. She stuck out her hand and held it inches from my hip.

"I am tatiana de la tierra," she announced haughtily.

I nodded and shook her hand, waiting for her to declare her mission.

"Um," she muttered. This tic showed a crack in her aggressive armor. "I wrote the book *For the Hard Ones*. You reviewed it for *Girlfriends Magazine*."

Ah! I thought to myself. *We are here for a reckoning!*

"Yes!" I agreed. I *had* written a critical review.

tatiana straightened her spine. "You gave the book...a B," she said. "I want to know...why a B?" She waited with a stern expression.

I smiled inwardly. "I only wrote the copy for the reviews. My editor assigned the letter grades. *She* chose the B."

tatiana relaxed into forgiveness. "Will you sign my book?" she asked and thrust my book at me.

"Sure," I answered, glancing up at her as I inscribed it.

As I handed back the book, I understood where I stood: in the presence of a perfectionist with huge balls.

Gradually, tatiana and I developed a friendship. I learned to associate courage with her. This virtue fueled tatiana's craft as well as many of her day-to-day choices. tatiana found writing *For the Hard Ones* challenging and the book, therefore, may be regarded as an epistemic experiment in queer courage.

As a lesbian phenomenologist, tatiana requires a tailored method of interpretation, a lesbian HERmeneutics. The following questions, to which I've proposed my own answers, might guide such an exegesis:

Q) Who is the lesbian author?
As she was known to bark in Spanish during roll calls: "¡tatiana de la tierra...presente!"
Q) What is the lesbian subject matter of the text?
First-lesbian (as opposed to first-person) consciousness
Q) Why did a lesbian write this text?
Curiosity, courage, and Sapphic eros inspired its authorship
Q) How did a lesbian compose this text?
By using her tongue as her pen
Q) When did a lesbian compose this text?
All lesbian events occur according to lesbian time
Q) In what lesbian place was this text written?
Texas
Q) By what lesbian means was this text published?
A) Lesbian scheming brought this text into the light.

tatiana's canon inspires a yonic, not phallic, reading. In her hands, language became hard, wet, soft and cleft. Sentences became surprise-filled cunts. To experience their surprises, one must be willing to treat cunts as mouths, interlocutors and oracles.

The tongue occupies an equally important place in tatiana's canon, it exists as the cunt's complement, and it holds an almost deified status as exemplified by the poem Lengua Alabanza: "All praise be to tongue..."

For the Hard Ones is structured according to tongue. tatiana translated each phenomenology from English to Spanish and this bilingual format mirrors the lesbian gender switching exhibited within the phenomenologies. The female abstractions that populate *For the Hard Ones* translate their lesbianism into femme or butch existences and this duality suggests the existence of two mother tongues that form, and propagate, a lesbian language family.

The accumulated effect of tongue references throughout tatiana's canon further underscores the primacy of bilingual experience. In some poems, tongues are forked. In other writings, Spanglish doubles the tongue by tripling it. tatiana dubbed the tongue "the lesbian mascot," and she packed her odes to it with sensual onomateopoeia that required those who read it aloud to perform oral gymnastics. tatiana's fertile treatment of the tongue insinuates infinity: we may fork the tongue over and over forever and still not run out of morphemes. Linguistic pleasure and challenge remain eternally ripe.

Myriam Gurba

Introduction: Una mujer peligrosa

tatiana de la tierra was a dangerous woman. She loved smut and worshipped the cunt. She was wild, fat, free, and fearless. She wrote odes to unsavory bearded lesbians and celebrated fleshy women with violated vaginas and "fallen tits" who "fuck joyfully."[1] This was her gift, to topple patriarchy and transform the world she wrote and lived in into a lyrical lesbian fuckfest where dykes, mermaids, goddess worshippers, and puta raps reigned supreme.

Born in Villavicencio, Colombia, tatiana de la tierra migrated to Miami, Florida with her family at the age of seven in 1968. In her autobiographical essay, "Wings," she describes being torn away from the familiar, her grandmothers, great aunts, aunts, the Andean mountains, and the experience of living on a farm where eggs were collected and where arepas were made daily at the crack of dawn.[2]

In contrast, Miami was a place of seismic shifts, where landscape, culture, food, and particularly language were unstable for tatiana, as they often are for so many newly arrived immigrants. As one of only a few Spanish speakers at her elementary school, her sense of "otherness" as a newcomer and as an English learner pissed her off and propelled her forward. "I dreaded those public moments that highlighted the fact that I was a foreigner. Sometimes I sat at my desk, plotting my revenge. I would master the English language. I

---

1 The phrases "a dangerous woman," "fallen tits," and "fuck joyfully" are taken from de la tierra's poem "Paint Me a Dangerous Woman," which originally appeared in Spanish in her chapbook by the same name (Buffalo, Nueva York: Chibcha Press, 2004). The English version of the poem later appeared in *Tierra 2010: poems, songs, & a little blood* (Long Beach, California: Chibcha, Press, 2010).

2 tatiana de la tierra, "Wings." In *Without a Net: The Female Experience of Growing Up Working Class*. Ed. Michelle Tea (Emeryville: Seal Press, 2004): 91-96. Republished in La Bloga on July 30, 2017. https://labloga.blogspot.com/2017/07/wings-by-tatiana-de-la-tierra.html

would infiltrate the gringo culture without letting on that I was a traitor. I would battle in their tongue and make them stumble. I would cut out their souls and leave them on the shore to be pecked on by vultures."[3]

tatiana began writing in English as a teenager, and while she learned to slay linguistic dragons with her pen, she often noted that her love of literature began much sooner. In a 2009 blog post, she shared, "My mom handed me over to a world of words when she read me poetry as a child. She read me children's poems and prose by the brilliant Colombian author Rafael Pombo, and she also read me Neruda and Benedetti. She blasted music and sang along while doing housework, knitting and reading, introducing me to bambucos, boleros, and baladas, gifting me with music and melody. I took it from there. I was a budding writer in junior high when I published my first haiku in the school's literary newsletter. By high school I was writing feature articles and editing the school paper. I discovered the power of the word by listening, reading, and finally, writing."[4]

In the 1980s, when she was in her twenties, tatiana came out as a lesbian and began writing with a Latina lesbian focus. She wrote in English, Spanish, and Spanglish. This polyamorous lingualism she considered, like her sexuality, entirely natural. tatiana was fascinated by translation. She translated an entire manuscript by her favorite poet Cristina Peri Rossi, *Estrategias del deseo*, with the permission of the author. She regularly created faithless translations of her own work (often with the help of her mother), caring more about meaning, style and the rhythm of words than being literal. She was not into the tedium of pampering monolingual audiences nor was she a fan of side-by-side translations. The first publishing of *For The Hard Ones / Para Las Duras* (Calaca Press and Chibcha Press 2002) was a flip book where the Spanish and English existed as two separate mini-books

---

3 Ibid.

4 "Guest Colomunist: Olga Garcia, tatiana de la tierra, Liz Vega." July 26, 2009. *La Bloga*. https://labloga.blogspot.com/2009/07/guest-columnists-olga-garcia-tatiana-de.html

bound into one. Side by side translations are also extremely rare in tatiana's self-publishing endeavors. For the republishing of *For The Hard Ones,* Sinister Wisdom proposed side-by-side translations for several practical reasons. We consulted tatiana's runes and trust she has granted us her permission (if not, at least her forgiveness) for the side-by-side translations in this project. She was, after all, a firm believer in the art of juxtaposition and reviving creative work but not of rehashing it in the same exact way.

As a budding dyke in the 80s, tatiana began publishing her work mostly in fliers, magazines, and Latina lesbian anthologies. The publications to feature some of her earliest works were *Compañeras*; *Gay and Lesbian Poetry in Our Time*; *Visibilities; Ms. Magazine; Latino Stuff Review; Lesbian Contradiction;* and *Sinister Wisdom.* Still, limited visibility and publishing opportunities for Latina lesbians left her hungry for more. The mainstream literary world was predominately white, straight, and English-only. The alternative publishing worlds also left a lot to be desired. Despite the hard fought gains of the Black/Brown/Red Power movements as well as the feminist and queer crusades of the 60s and 70s, the alternative publishing worlds, like the social movements that created them, often sought social justice in silos that created multiple exclusions for dykes of color. ¡Tortura!

What to do if you were someone like tatiana de la tierra who in the 80's and 90's wanted, for instance, to publish a queer dictionary of Latin American pussy? In Spanglish? With an international distribution? Like the true trailblazer that she was, tatiana shunned the idea of begging for a seat at the existing exclusionary literary table(s). Instead, she identified the hunger that queers of color had and created sumptuous literary and publishing feasts where Latina lesbians were placed center-stage and center-page.

In the early 1990s, tatiana co-founded, co-edited, and co-published two groundbreaking magazines, *esto no tiene nombre* and *conmoción,* which featured the bilingual musings of Latina lesbian writers. The herstory of these trailblazing magazines is explored in detail by Sara Gregory in her essay, "*Esto no tiene nombre* and *conmoción*: revistas for the hard ones," later in this collection. We pause at the magazines here briefly only to note that it was via *esto* and *conmocion* that tatiana came to be an activist writer for what she called "la causa," specifically the cause of publishing the poems/stories/relatos and, most importantly, the orgasms of Latina lesbians both in the United States and in Latin America. In fact, her literary and political lesbian revolution crossed borders across the continent wherever women gathered to shed the shackles of heteropatriarchy and revel in their freedom while smashing imperialism. At these freedom-making experiments, from the Michigan Womyns Music Festival to many Latin American and Caribbean Lesbian Feminist Encuentros (and Feminist Encuentros), tatiana found comrades, lovers, and friends to build new lesbian cultures of liberation. She trafficked in her special brand of what she called "lesbian smut," doing readings and selling chapbooks from North America to the tierra del fuego and attending book fairs and literary festivals to smuggle sexually subversive treasures back home.

Not only was she a luchadora of the Latina and Latin American lesbiana literary scene, tatiana was a relentless warrior in her own life. At the age of 29, she was diagnosed with lupus, an illness she sometimes attributed to having grown up a mile away from a nuclear power plant in Homestead, Florida.

From the age of 29 until her death in her early 50s, the illness was an unexpected mine field that turned her body into the "última guerra mundial" ("last world war") sending her into hospitals across the US, to healers in the mountains of Colombia, to alternative health practitioners in the desert of New Mexico, to Chile where she communed with ayahausca and shamans, and to experimental healing clinics across the border into Tijuana.[5] For tatiana, the body was a battleground where illness and pleasure constantly brawled and also remarkably co-existed. After one experimental procedure that involved transplanting pig tissue, she described herself in a poem, "I, Snow Mermaid," as "heart

---

5 The phrase "mi cuerpo, última guerra mundial." comes from her poem "Mi luna es un abanico" *Píntame una mujer peligrosa* (Chibcha Press, Buffalo, Nueva York. 2004): 14.

twitching / blood on cutting board / cells on ice / I, pig woman / snorting orgasms dancing / death..."[6]

Despite reoccurring illness and hospitalizations throughout her adult life, as well as countless campaigns of alternative healing protocols and walking numerous spiritual paths seeking healing, tatiana managed to do two extraordinary things that are clearly reflected in her literary work: maintain agency ,and make of her body a temple where pleasure and beauty were redefined, radicalized, and queerified.

In 1996, after a near-death experience, tatiana shifted her focus from publishing to nurturing her own creative work. She moved to El Paso, Texas to fulfill a literary dream, to complete an MFA in creative writing. Her classic introduction to fellow UTEP classmates and instructors, "Hi. My name is tatiana de la tierra. I write cunt stories." It was in the border region of El Paso/Juarez, among sprouting cactus and flying roaches, with the notorious femicides of Juarez as constant backdrop, that tatiana wrote *For The Hard Ones*. tatiana narrates the birth of *For The Hard Ones* in her enclosed essay, "On Phenomenological Herstory." She credits as creative springboard Dante Medina's *Zonas de la escritura* and a writing assignment given by her Mexican literature professor Dr. Fernando García Nuñez. He had required a literary criticism survey paper, which tatiana hated and, therefore, resisted. Typical of tatiana, she used her persuasive powers to propose an alternative assignment for herself, and once given the green light, she wrote her way into the "Zonas de las lesbianas" ("Lesbian Zones"), the original title of her manuscript.

After completion of her MFA, tatiana went on to complete her Master of Library of Sciences at the University of Buffalo, where she then worked as an academic librarian. Her work in librarianship, both at the University of Buffalo and later at the Inglewood Public Library in California, focused on making Latin American and queer texts more visible and accessible, and drew attention to the

---

6 tatiana de la tierra, "I, Snow Mermaid." *Tierra 2010: poems, songs, & a little blood* (Chibcha Press, Long Beach, California, 2010). Poem appears on the inside of the back cover and is not listed on the table of contents.

political struggles of Latinxs in the US. While she wrote critical academic articles about the racial/sexual politics of cataloguing, she also continued to write and publish her stories poems, songs, interviews, and blogs.

Working at the University at Buffalo, she befriended Latinx graduate students in English and Modern Languages, and with Bobby Lopez and Lorna Pérez founded the Salon de Belleza, a weekly writing group that focused on poetry, politics, and the unapologetic pursuit of beautiful, raw, creative expression. The salon membership swelled to upwards of 25 people and met weekly for many years in the early 2000s, and ultimately led to tatiana creating Chibcha Press, which published chapbooks, including her own work *Porcupine Love: Tales from my Papaya (2003),* as well as the work of salon writers Lorna Pérez (*Overdetermined Romances, 2003)* and Anna Reckin (*Spill,* 2004). In true tatiana fashion, all of Chibcha's chapbooks were envisioned as art objects, featuring brightly colored papers, vellum inserts, hand beaded bindings, images, and photographs, most famously nude underwater author photos.

Wherever tatiana moved, she took with her Chibcha Press. She continued to self-publish her own work and support other women writers with her press until the end of her life. She also carried with her the spirit of creating community with fellow writers. In Long Beach, California, where she resettled in 2007 after a psychic advised her that she align with the vibration of the land there, she co-founded *The Tongue Fisters* (a queer women of color writing collective), and participated in *Las Guayabas* (a Latina writing collective). In Long Beach, she went on to publish three more chapbooks of poetry, as well as a children's book, *Xía y las mil sirenas.*

tatiana de la tierra left us way too soon. In May of 2012, in Long Beach, California, tatiana was diagnosed with stage four cancer. There were complications due to lupus and failing kidneys, (she'd been on dialysis for a couple of years), so chemotherapy was not an option. After her diagnosis, tatiana did things entirely her way. In the years leading up to her diagnosis, she had dreamt of opening an ecoaldea – part ecosphere part commune – in the mountains of Colombia. Despite her diagnosis, tatiana continued to dream and plan her escape. She ultimately chose hospice, but not without calling in her own clan of healers and shamans. She gave herself an alter ego and name, Suerte Sirena. She cleared energy with palo santo and sage. She got herself an infrared sauna. She pulled runes and consulted psychics. She took a surplus of supplements. She ate superfoods. She dabbed on essential oils with names that lured, *Romance, Flirtation, Passion.* She posted selfies from her bed on Facebook, asking who was going to adopt her two beloved cats, Shakira and Mojito. She lay in bed with friends reading poetry and communed with her rocks and crystals. She stayed up late at night with her girlfriend, Cristy, dream-talking about everything they were still going to do.

tatiana's mother, Fabiola, came to Long Beach from Miami, Florida during those last months to care for her. tatiana's aunts, tía Gladys and tía Lulu, along with other relatives, came all the way from Colombia for extended visits. The rest of us who gathered around tatiana during those final months were a mishmash of queer and straight, bilingual, multi-racial, immigrant and native born. All of us had come to know and love tatiana in one way or another through the years. Friends and ex-lovers from farther distances also came, or if they could not come, they called, or emailed, or texted, or sent Facebook messages. We all had our own wacky or intimate stories about how we had met tatiana, and how she had at one point or another made us care for and feed her cats, or assemble Ikea furniture, or help her move this or fix that. She was a Diosa/Diva, after all, famous for building relationships by putting people to work and telling us all what to do. This did not change during the last months of her life, and we took up these tasks with love and a sense of urgency; we were honored to assist her in any way we could.

tatiana was a life-long archivist and collector of things. She safekept letters, family heirlooms, large plastic bins full of thousands of pictures, many of them of queer naked women from intimate settings as well as historic gatherings. Her home was a colorful museum of items that she had gathered from all her travels and from different epochs of her life. There was, among other eye-catching dazzling things, her collection of ceramic cunts; the altar of pineapples; the collection of records of women musicians from around the world; an epic collection of precious rocks and healing crystals; Botero; Frida; the flyers/zines/programs/posters/art by and about Latina Lesbians.

Amongst her most prized collections were her books and the archives of her own creative work and publishing projects. What would become of these archives when she was no longer on this earth to care for them herself? This was a primary concern to tatiana and she focused a good part of her energy at the end of her life on this task. We, along with the UCLA Chicano Resource Center where her archives are now housed, worked with her to sort through her papers and creative work. It was not uncommon during those last months to walk into tatiana's house and find her surrounded by boxes, weeding through things, instructing us, her helpers, what should be labeled what and what should go where. When encouraged to rest, she seemed almost offended. Time was running out and she had not dedicated her life to writing and publishing to let it collect dust and wither, or worse, to pass it on unorganized. Writing and publishing had been among tatiana's greatest enduring passions and these passions burned inside her until the very end.

We thank Julie Enszer and Sinister Wisdom for honoring the work and legacy of tatiana de la tierra in this wonderful republishing of *For The Hard Ones,* which includes in addition to the original manuscript, a foreword by Myriam Gurba, an important overview of the herstory of *esto no tiene nombre* and *conmoción* by Sara Gregory, and a reprinting of "El Regalo" ("The Gift") by Fabiola Restrepo, tatiana's mother.

The truth is, tatiana de la tierra not only feasted on the Latina lesbian word, she also wanted to feed us. tatiana de la tierra was and is, as writer Achy Obejas termed her, "a Sapphic warrior" who joyfully picked up the literary torch passed on by other queer women of color writers who helped pave the way for an empowered queer literary world, most notably women such as Audre Lorde, Barbara Smith, Cheryl Clark, Gloria Anzaldúa, and Cherríe Moraga, to name just a few.

To enter into the pages of *For The Hard Ones* is to enter the flesh. It is to wake up with the "smell of sex in our hair" in a world that is both material and mythical in its creation of a lesbo paradise.

To enter *For The Hard Ones* is to get tongued by tatiana de la tierra, Latina lesbian style, "con la lengua se dice: 'te voy a romper todita mami...'" ("with the tongue you can say, 'I'm going to eat you piece by piece.'")

This is tatiana's delectable offering to us all, full of Sapphic insight, bold bilingual flavors, lust and plenty of dream-dust.

May you savor and enjoy.

Olga García Echeverría & Maylei Blackwell

January 2018
under the Super Blue Blood Moon

Courtesy of the tatiana de la tierra private collection.

Las Fenomenologías
The Phenomenologies

Ser

no hacen falta los agujeros para encontrarlas. por cualquier andén pasan, a veces pareciéndose a cualquiera. también lucen de uniforme planchado con un emblema declaratorio. pero sin importar la facha, los ojos que las detallan conocen la imagen al instante y en silencio o en voz alta las declaran: Lesbianas.

pero ¿por qué son lesbianas?

esa respuesta es bien fácil. ¿Por qué navegan las nubes por el cielo y las soñadores por la tierra?

Being

you find them walking along on any sidewalk, sometimes seeming like the rest. or they may wear badges and starched uniforms, even colorful cardboard signs. yet regardless of their appearance, the eyes that scrutinize them know the image instantly, and in silence or out loud those eyes declare: lesbian.

but why are they lesbians?

why do clouds navigate the sky and why do dreamers wander on earth?

Cuando se dice "soy"

cuando digo que soy lesbiana me adelanto a los que, al referirse a mi, dicen: "es". al ser lo que que soy, también sigo siendo todo lo que soy: la que desayuna con toronjas, la que no se peina nunca, la que baila vallenatos y la que sigue siendo lo que es.

la que "es" pero no dice "soy" nada más puede ser lo que es cuando está rodeada de otras que posiblemente tampoco dicen lo que son salvo cuando están entre ellas mismas.

la que "es" pero no dice "soy" también puede "ser" lo que es cuando está sola, cuando no hay ojos para detallarla y declararla.

claro que no importa si las que son no dicen "soy" porque igual casi siempre se sabe que son.

When I Say "I am"

when I say that I am a lesbian I get ahead of those who refer to me by saying: she is. when I am what I am, I continue to be everything that I am: the one who eats grapefruits for breakfast, who never brushes her hair, who dances vallenatos, and who continues to be what she is.

the one who is but does not say "I am" can only be what she is when surrounded by others who also don't say that they are unless they are with each other.

the one who is and does not say "I am" can also be what she is by herself when there are no eyes around to scrutinize and label her.

still, it matters not that those who are do not say "I am" because in any case everyone else almost always knows that they are.

Soñando en lesbiano

puedo entrar a la mañana con los rasgos del sueño eterno: vivir en un planeta de mujeres. es puro canto y caricias sobre lomas lilas y bosques fértiles. nos bañamos bajo cascadas de aguas claras, y así, desnudas y mojadas, nos montamos las unas a las otras. nuestro deseo en una ballena que encuentra la calma en lo profundo del mar.

huelo sexo en mi pelo al amanecer.

el olor del sueño me perfuma todos los días. voy al correo a buscar estampillas con dibujos de flores o frutas para enviar cartas a las mujeres que caminaron conmigo sobre suelos de musgo húmedo.

estamos en un mundo que no es nuestro. ¿qué hacemos con los sueños que juegan en la subconciencia cada noche?

puede ser que nuestro planeta de mujeres sea no más que un sueño. ¿pero quién dice que las imágenes de las noches no son tan reales como las de que los días? nadie sabe cuántas nos bañamos en los bosques ni quiénes volamos con el cuerpo abierto. y no es para que lo sepan. afortunadamente, el paraíso siempre lo soñamos, lo hacemos nuestro. ahí nos encontramos y vivimos un recuerdo colectivo.

entonces, huele a sexo mi pelo al amanecer.

Dreaming of Lesbos

I can enter the morning with traces of an eternal dream: to live on a planet of women. we sing in the fertile forest, caress on lavender hills, bathe beneath cascades of clear waters. and just like that, nude and wet, we mount each other's bodies. our desire is a whale that searches for calm in the depth of the sea.

I smell sex in my hair when I awaken.

the dream perfumes all of my days. I go to the post office and look for stamps with etchings of flowers and fruits so that I can send letters to the women who loved me in my sleep.

we are in a world that is not ours. what do we do with the dreams that touch our consciousness in the nude each night?

our planet of women is nothing more than a dream. who knows how many of us bathe in the woods or which ones of us have wings that let us fly with our flesh? it's not for anyone to know. fortunately, we always dream paradise, we make it ours. there, we find each other and live in our collective memory.

and so, I smell sex in my hair when I awaken.

El arte de mariposear

las lesbianas somos un arte. en algún momento somos las que aparentamos ser—estudiantes, anarquistas, amas de casa, poetas—y en otro somos un reinvento que no tiene nada que ver con lo que éramos. nos hacemos mecánicas, paganas, bibliotecarias, lesbianas.

las transformaciones son cada vez más bellas. somos mujeres mariposeadas.

el arte lleva a los espectadores a una dimensión que, antes del arte, no se conocía por los que no admiran el mundo más allá del blanco y el negro. lo que parecía ser la realidad se deshace: el ataúd es una cueva de placer, la manzana es una bomba, el globo del ojo es una mandala.

la deconstrucción de los significados comunes y corrientes le abre camino al cambio. si el ataúd es una cueva de placer ¿no será bienvenida la muerte? si una manzana es una bomba ¿debería consumir una en el desayuno? si el ojo es una mandala ¿será que la paz interna se encuentra en los centros de los ojos?

este cambio es lo que conduce a la evolución. el ama de casa se convierte en una lesbiana radical separatista, y ésta se vuelve pacifista, luego se hace madre, se reinvente artista, deviene en alcohólica, se torna camionera, se vuelve padre, se rehace feminista, se hace quien sea que quiera hasta que ella decide, algún día, hacerse mariposa.

para el arte lesbiano no se requieren pinturas ni pinceles ni marcos ni telas. la ruptura con identidades que parecían eternas es suficiente para mariposear. con re-nombrar lo que fue y será, se acaba con lo que era y hubiera sido.

las transformaciones son cada día más bellas. somos mujeres mariposeadas.

The Art of Butterflying

lesbianism is an art form. one moment we are who we seem to be—a student, an anarchist, a housewife, a poet—and then we create that which seems to have nothing to do with who we are. we become mechanics, pagans, librarians, lesbians.

the transformations are more beautiful every time. we are but butterflied women.

art brings a dimension to its spectators that, before art, was not experienced by those who do not admire the world beyond black and white. what appears to be reality is broken: the coffin is a pleasure cove; the apple a bomb; the eyeball, a mandala.

the deconstruction of common meanings opens the path to change. if the coffin is a pleasure cove, is death not welcome? if an apple is a bomb, should I have one for breakfast? if the eyeball is a mandala, does inner peace reside in the centers of our eyes?

change leads to evolution. the housewife becomes a radical lesbian separatist who becomes a pacifist, who becomes a mother, who becomes a housewife, who becomes an artist, who becomes an alcoholic, who becomes a truck driver, who becomes a father, who becomes a feminist, who becomes whoever else she wants to, until she decides, one day, to become a butterfly.

lesbian art requires no paint brushes on canvas. the rupture with identities that seemed forever real and true is sufficient for butterflying. by re-creating who we were and re-naming who we are, we let go of what would have been and become another invention of ourselves.

the transformations are more beautiful every time. we are butterflied women.

Una lesbiana, por partes

las manos: representan el placer; deben invitar con suavidad y brillo. el corte y decoración de las uñas depende de los deseos íntimos; las lesbianas se unen por las uñas.

la mirada: las lesbianas se claven con la vista; se miran directamente y así se penetran. los ojos de lesbianas contienen la historia que jamás se cuenta. por eso es que indagan y reciben respuestas sin palabra alguna.

el andar: caminan con confianza; cada paso tiene un propósito que ya se ha determinado. no importa si andan descalzas o con botas o tacones. igual, hacen tronar la tierra bajo los pies y muchos le temen a su andar.

los atuendos: dicen que las lesbianas usan el vestuario que le pertenece a otros. pero como ellas son dueñas de sí mismas cualquier prenda que se pongan califica como vestuario de lesbiana. una lesbiana se puede vestir con Calvin Kleins o panties de encaje, con un abrigo de lana o una capa de Robin Hood, con tacones o botas de combate, con camisa de franela o falda hindú, con cuernos de diablo o con alas translúcidas. las lesbianas se visten como quieren.

los dedos: se clasifican como órganos vitales.

todas estas partes pueden existir aparte la una de la otra, pero tienen que estar todas presentes para formar parte de una lesbiana.

A Lesbian, By Parts

the hands: representing pleasure, they should invite with softness and shine. the style and décor of the nails depends on intimate desires; lesbians unite through their fingernails.

the look: captivating—they look directly inside and penetrate each other. lesbian eyes contain the history that is never spoken and so they can ask questions and receive answers without a word.

the walk: confident—each strep has a predetermined purpose. they could be barefoot or wearing flip-flops or high-heeled boots. in any case, lesbians make the earth thunder beneath their feet and are feared by many who encounter them on the way.

the dress: they say that some lesbians dress in a way that belongs to others. but since they are the owners of themselves, anything lesbians wear qualifies as lesbian attire: transcluent wings, ripped jeans, executive suits, parachute pants, Calvin Kleins, hoops skirts, strap-ons. lesbians dress as they please.

the fingers: classified as vital organs.

all of these parts can exist apart from one another, but they all have to be present to form part of a lesbian.

La mujer y la lesbiana:
El cuerpo y el alma

se habla mucho, en las escuelas donde se enseña el lesbianismo, de la diferencia entre una mujer y una lesbiana.

¿no son todas las lesbianas mujeres? y aunque no todas las mujeres son lesbianas ¿no es posible que cualquier mujer sea lesbiana?

y dado que hay mujeres que son lesbianas ¿cómo se diferencian estas lesbianas (que son mujeres) de las mujeres (que son o no son lesbianas)?

la cosa se complica cuando los términos empleados no son mujer y lesbiana, sino mujer y macha, manflora, maricona, tortillera, arepera, pata, patlache, invertida, jota, lila, pasiva, activa y cualquier otro montón de palabras que significan que una lesbiana no es una mujer.

pero ¿qué es una "mujer"? de acuerdo al Pequeño Larousse: *Hembra, persona del sexo femenino de la especie humana 2. Persona adulta del sexo femenino de la especie humana 3. Esposa*

igual a las mujeres, las lesbianas son hembras y pertenecen al sexo femenino.

igual a las mujeres, las lesbianas pueden ser esposas de lesbianas o de no-lesbianas. una lesbiana puede ser la "propiedad" de otra, si éste es su deseo. igualmente, lesbianas pueden ser maridos, papis, dueños de su "mujer". o sea, una lesbiana puede ser esposa, y también puede tener una esposa (o varias).

una "lesbiana" es: *Mujer homosexual.*

una "homosexual" es: *Dícese de la persona que siente atracción sexual por individuos de su mismo sexo.*

las lesbianas, por definición, son mujeres. pero existen tremendas diferencias entre las mujeres y las lesbianas que jamás se encuentran dentro de un diccionario.

suele decirse que las lesbianas tenemos el cuerpo de mujer pero con alma de lesbiana.

así que las lesbianas si son mujeres, pero la mayor parte de las lesbianas son lesbianas.

The Woman and the Lesbian: The Body and The Soul

there is much talk, in the schools where lesbianism is learned, of the difference between a woman and a lesbian.

but aren't all lesbians women? and although all women are not lesbians, isn't it possible that any woman could become a lesbian?

and given that there are women who are lesbians, how do you differentiate between these lesbians (who are women) and women (who are not lesbians)?

things get complicated when the terms used are not "woman" and "lesbian" but rather "woman" and: womon, dyke, mack daddy, bulldagger, gay, butch, queer, femme, family, patlache, lipstick lesbian, top, bottom, girlie girl, combat femme and many other words that suggest that a lesbian is not a woman.

but what is a "woman"? according to the dictionary: *Female, person of the feminine sex of the human species. 2. Adult person of the feminine sex of the human species. 3. Wife.*

like women, lesbians are females and belong to the feminine sex.

lesbians can also be wives of lesbians or of non-lesbians. a lesbian can be owned, if she chooses to be, if it is her desire. likewise, lesbians can also be husbands, owners of women, of their "woman". and so, like women, a lesbian can be a wife, and, unlike women, a lesbian can have a wife.

a "lesbian": *Female homosexual.*

a "homosexual":   *Said of a person who feels sexual attraction for individuals of the same sex.*

it is clear that all lesbians are, by definition, women. yet there are tremendous differences between women and lesbians that will never be found in any dictionary!

it is enough to say that lesbians have the body of a woman, yet the soul of a lesbian.

and so it is that lesbians are women but, mostly, lesbians are lesbians.

L@s otr@s de nosotr@s: Entre comillas

hay "mujeres" que nacieron "hembras" que son "mujeres" "lesbianas".

hay "mujeres" que nacieron "hembras" que son "lesbianas" no-"mujeres".

hay "mujeres" que nacieron no-"mujeres" que se hicieron "mujeres" y son "lesbianas".

hay "lesbianas" que nacieron "hembras" y se hicieron no-"mujeres" (y siguen siendo "lesbianas").

hay "mujeres" que parecen no-"mujeres" y son no-"lesbianas".

hay "mujeres" que bautizan "lesbianas" que también son no-"lesbianas".

hay "mujeres" que son casi-"lesbianas"—lo sueñan, lo intentan, pero no son capaces.

hay "lesbianas" que son Lesbianas.

The "Others" of Us

there are "women" who were born "female" who are "lesbian" "women".

there are "women" who were born "female" who are non-"feminine" "lesbians".

there are "women" who were born not-"women" who became "women" and are "lesbians".

there are "lesbians" who were born "female" and who became not-"women" (and continue being "lesbians").

there are "women" who baptize themselves as "lesbians" who are also non-"lesbians".

there are "women" who are almost "lesbians"—they fantasize about being with "women" and they experiment, to no avail; they are not capable of being "lesbians".

there are "lesbains" who are Lesbians.

Bitácora de la lesbiana

el camino hacia el lesbianismo implica renunciar al camino que ya estaba escrito. todo lo que debería ser y hacer se reemplaza con todo lo que da la gana.

en el fondo, ser lesbiana es un cambio de mano de poder. es cierto que el poder siempre nos pertenece, pero muchas veces se les permite a otros manejarlo. la lesbiana reclama su poder.

la ceremonia de iniciación al lesbianismo es un matrimonio con una misma. se camina sola hacia el altar, vestida con el traje de la piel. con cada paso se deja el destino que nunca fue propio y se acerca al que sí lo será. a la entrada de la puerta del lesbianismo se detiene. entonces se promete ser fiel a sí misma, se besa y se abraza su propio cuerpo.

así es que se entra, desnuda y enamorada, al lesbianismo.

Pathway to Lesbianism

the path to lesbianism implies the renunciation of the path that was already written. everything that you should be and do is replaced with what strikes your fancy.

being a lesbian is a changing of the hands of power. it is true that the power is always ours but many times we allow others to manage it for us. a lesbian reclaims her power.

the ceremony of initiation is a wedding with oneself. walk towards the altar, alone and dressed with the gown of your skin. with each step you leave behind the destiny that was never your own and you get close to that which will be of your making. detain yourself at the entrance to the door of lesbianism. promise to be faithful to yourself, kiss and embrace your own body.

that is how you enter lesbianism: naked and in love.

¿Quién es la que dice "yo soy"?

decirlo de verdad—yo soy lesbiana—es declarar la huella que deja el hecho de ser lesbiana. como consecuencia, no hay campo para cuestionar. a nadie se le ocurre preguntarse: ¿será?

hablar de las que son, como si se estuviera contando algo aparte de lo que uno es, requiere distancia de una misma. a la vez, como las mentiras siempre se intuyen, la gente se pregunta: ¿será?

no es tan fácil distinguir entre la que dice "soy" y la que no dice nada. la que compra un ramo de claveles rosados en el supermercado para su amada es igual a la que lo recibe. una puede ser la que dice lo que es y la otra puede ser la que lo niega, pero dentro del acto de la flor y el amor, son lo mismo: lesbianas.

la que recibe las flores se acuerda de las dalias y margaritas que crecían en el patio de su tía cuando era niña. en los domingos preparaban varios ramos de flores para llevarlos a la tumba de la abuelita. atravesaba el pueblo con la tía mientras los ramos entre sus brazos le picaban la cara. a mitad del camino al cementerio paraban a tomar avena con buñuelos de los que vendían en carritos ambulantes. ¡qué nostalgia! mientras tanto su amada espera un beso, algún apretón, y se imagina la noche de vino, música y pasión que van a vivir.

siguen siendo distintas en cuanto a lo que se dice o se miente pero en la cama, ambas son lesbianas.

la que dice que es, reclama su realidad; la que no dice reclama su infidelidad.

Who Is the One Who Says "I am"?

to speak the truth—I am a lesbian—is to name the imprint that being a lesbian leaves. as a consequence, there is no space for questioning. no one will ask: is she?

to silence or deny the truth is to leave a trail of lies. people will surely ask: is she?

distinguishing between the one who says "I am" and the one who says nothing at all is not as simple as it appears. the one who buys carnations in the supermarket for her lover is the same as the one who will receive them. one can declare what she is and the other can deny it, but in the act of flowers and love, they are the same: lesbians.

the one who receives the flowers remembers the anthuriums that grew in her aunt's yard when she was a child. they brought flowers to the cemetery on Sundays. she rubs the carnations in her face and remembers the anthuriums that tickled her under the nose as she walked across town with her aunt. half-way there, they stopped for snacks from the carts on the streets. what nostalgia! meanwhile, her lover awaits a kiss, a squeeze, and imagines the night of wine, music and passion that they will share.

they continue to be different with regard to what they reveal or hide, but in the act of sex and love, they are the same: lesbians.

the one who says she is claims her reality; the other, her infidelity to her lesbian self.

Las formas de las lesbianas

ser lesbiana es una elección. al tomar esta identificación se eliminan las otras formas posibles; la ausencia de estas otras formas es lo que le da forma a la lesbiana.

ser lesbiana es un destino. al aceptar esta fortuna se eliminan las otras formas posibles; la ausencia de estas otras formas es lo que le da forma a la lesbiana.

las lesbianas dibujan su forma con las fronteras que mantienen a toda hora; son fronteras impenetrables.

la forma de la lesbiana es la pieza perdida del rompecabezas—es la pieza que jamás encuentra su lugar. como ella es dueña de su figura, la lesbiana no figura en el paisaje con el resto de las piezas.

por eso es que la lesbiana toma forma: porque es su propia propiedad.

Forms of Lesbians

being a lesbian is a choice. by opting for this identification you eliminate other possible forms. the absence of those other forms is what gives a lesbian form.

being a lesbian is a destiny. by accepting this fate you eliminate other possible forms. the absence of those forms is what gives a lesbian form.

lesbians draw their form with boundaries that they maintain at all hours, boundaries with impenetrable borders.

the lesbian form is the lost piece of the puzzle—the piece that will never fit, because lesbians do not fit in with the scenery of the other pieces.

this is why lesbians take form: because they belong to no one but themselves. they are their own property.

Nosotras y ellos

en el idioma lesbiano se dice que ellos: "se dieron cuenta", "fueron testigos de un abrazo", "vieron que había una cama para dos mujeres", "saben, y sabemos que lo saben", "no quieren saber y no queremos contarles".

estas son referencias de los otros que se fijan en nosotras.

en el idioma lesbiano se dice que ellas: "se jalaron los pelos", "se decidieron amar", "decidieron prohibir".

estas son referencias de nosotras sobre nosotras.

Us and Them: References

lesbians say: "they noticed," "they witnessed an embrace,"
"they saw that there was one bed for two women," "they know
and we know that they know," "they don't want to know and we
don't want to tell them."

these are references by us about them.

among lesbians we say: "we decided to love," "we pulled out
our hairs," "we decided to prohibit."

these are references about us by ourselves.

Los otros, las otras y nosotras

los que inventan las leyes, los que controlan la prensa, los que construyen las escaleras del éxito económico, los que determinan los procedimientos permitidos con nuestros cuerpos, los que penetran sin permiso, los que juzgan—éstos son los otros.

las que siguen todas las leyes, las que le dan la última palabra a la prensa popular, las que se limitan a seguir los caminos que limitan su economía, las que hacen con su cuerpo nada más que lo que se les permite hacer, las que se dejan penetrar sin opinar, las que se dejan juzgar—éstas son las otras.

las que se inventan sus leyes, las que publican sus propias palabras, las que salen del camino predeterminado para la sobrevivencia, las que deciden qué hacer con su propio cuerpo, las que penetran bienvenidas, las que no necesitan juez—éstas somos nosotras.

Us and Them: Laws of Desire

the ones who invent the laws, the ones who own the press, who impose economic systems, who determine the procedures allowed with our bodies, who penetrate without permission, who judge—those are them.

the ones who follow every law, who have faith in the press, who limit themselves to systems that limit their economy, who do with their bodies only as allowed, who are passively penetrated, who let themselves be judged—those are them.

the ones who write their own laws, who publish their own words, who create their own way to economic survival, who do with their bodies as they wish, who choose to welcome penetration and to penetrate, who need no judge—those are us.

Dime cómo tienes los labios y te diré quién eres

hay lesbianas duras.

éstas son las que se ponen los pantalones y a veces ni se los quitan. éstas son las peligrosas. las machas. las que se montan. las que cogen. las que muerden. las que penetran. las que dominan. las que todo el mundo sabe lo que son.

éstas son las más excitantes. saben entonar el deseo de una mujer. saben cómo hablarle a las tetas, cómo persuadir a los pezones. saben el significado de cada sonido. saben acariciar y agarrar y comer. saben engatusar gritos y calmar ansias. saben cómo endurecer una clítoris y además, saben qué hacer con ella.

hay lesbianas muñecas.

éstas son las de los labios rosados y las uñas rojas. son las maquilladas y perfumadas. las femininas. las que se dejan montar. las que se dejan coger. las que se dejan morder, penetrar, dominar. las que no todo el mundo sabe lo que son.

éstas son las más excitables. saben soltar el deseo. saben cómo hablar con las tetas, cómo dar los pezones. saben calibrar cada sonido. saben dejarse acariciar y agarrar y comer. saben gritar y llorar. saben cómo dejar que le endurezcan su clítoris y además, saben que hacer con ella.

hay lesbianas arcilla.

éstas son las que se ponen los pantalones y se los dejan quitar. son las deportivas, las andróginas, la nueva generación. son las que se montan y se dejan montar. las que cogen y se dejan coger. las que muerden, penetran, dominan y se dejan hacer de todo también. las que todo el mundo cree, pero no está seguro de que son.

éstas son las más excitadas. cantan y bailan el deseo. se hablan con las tetas y se timbran de pezón a pezón. hacen ruidos y se acarician y se agarran y se comen simultáneamente. saben gritar y llorar, y saben hacer gritar y llorar a otra. saben endurecer y dejar que le endurezcan su clítoris y además, saben que hacer con ella.

Tell Me How You Decorate Your Lips And I'll Tell You Who You Are

some lesbians are hard.

they are the ones who wear the pants and never take them off. they are the dangerous ones. the butches. the ones who get on top. the ones who fuck. who bite. who penetrate. who dominate. the ones who everyone knows are dykes.

they are the most exciting. they know how to tune in to a woman's desire. they know how to speak to the breasts, how to persuade the nipples. they know the significance of each sound. they know how to caress and grab and eat. they know how to coax screams and calm anxieties. they know how to harden a clitoris and they know what to do with it once it's hard.

some lesbians are dolls.

they are the ones with matching plum lips and nails. they are the ones who are painted and perfumed. the feminine ones. the ones who like being on the bottom. who open themselves to be fucked. who long to be bitten, penetrated, dominated. the ones that not everyone knows are dykes.

they are the most excitable. they know how to submit to desire. they know how to speak with their tits, how to offer their nipples. how to calibrate each sound. how to let themselves be caressed, grabbed, eaten. they know how to scream and cry. they know how to let their clitoris harden and they know what to do with it once it's hard.

some lesbians are clay.

they are the ones who wear the pants and permit others take them off. they are the sporty ones, the androgynous, the new generation. they are the ones who get on top and on the bottom too. the ones who fuck and get fucked. the ones who bite, penetrate, and dominate and give themselves over for the same. the ones who everyone suspects without being certain of what they are.

they are the most excited. they sing and dance desire. they speak tit to tit, buzz themselves nipple to nipple. they make sounds and caress and grab and eat each other simultaneously. they know how to scream and cry. they know how to let their clitoris harden and how to harden another one's clitoris, and they know what to do with them once they're hard.

Sobre la lengua

¿por qué no admitir que la lengua es la mascota preferida de las lesbianas?

con la lengua se dice: "te voy a romper todita mami", "preciosa preciosa que te quiero diosa", "¿y estas tetas las mandaste a hacer para mí?"

con la lengua se hace: una bandeja entrepiernas, un jalón de cuerpo y alma, trueno y relámpago en la base de la garganta, un manjar privado, orgasmos múltiples, silencio como ojo de huracán, una orquesta sinfónica lesbiana.

con la lengua se dicen y se hacen muchas más cosas,   ¿pero para qué contarlas todas?

datos sobre los hechos lingüísticos lésbicos se encuentran, sublingual, en los Archivos de la Lengua. las únicas que tienen acceso a estos documentos son las que meten la lengua.

es gracias a la lengua que existen las lesbianas, pero no es únicamente con la lengua que se hace una lesbiana.

About the Tongue

why not admit that the tongue is the lesbian mascot?

with the tongue you can say: "I'm going to eat you piece by piece."

with the tongue you can make: a platter between the legs, a direct connection between the body and soul, thunder and lightning at the base of the throat, a private dish, multiple orgasms, silence from the eye of a hurricane, a lesbian symphonic orchestra.

with the tongue you can say and make many more things, but why reveal them all?

information about lesbian linguistic deeds can be found, sublingual, in the Archives of the Tongue. the only ones who have access to these documents are the ones who are guided by the tip of their tongue.

it is thanks to the tongue that there are lesbians, but it is not only with the tongue that a lesbian is a lesbian.

La penetración

la lesbiana que penetra a su mujer corre el riesgo de perderse adentro;   el sonido interno del volcán es un arrullo.   ¿hasta dónde puede entrar?

la que abre las piernas y se deja penetrar también corre el riesgo de perderse adentro; la tienen cautiva en la libertad. ¿hasta dónde puede volar?

así es que las dos son prisioneras de la penetración.

es tan fuerte que hace llorar a cualquier mujer fuerte. la penetración derrumba rascacielos, derrite cerraduras, descubre verdades.

la penetración es un acto literario. con ella se escribe *La doctrina de la putería, La ley del deseo, Un nuevo catecismo de las piernas bien abiertas.*

la penetración es un acto bendito.

Penetration

the lesbian who penetrates her woman runs the risk of getting lost inside; the internal sound of a volcano is a lullaby. how far can she enter?

the ones who opens her legs for penetration also runs the risk of losing herself inside; she is held captive in liberty. how far can she fly?

this is how both of them are prisoners of penetration.

penetration is so powerful it makes a strong woman cry; penetrating demolishes skyscrapers, melts dead bolts, discovers truths.

penetration is a literary act. *The Doctrine of Sluts, The Law of Desire, A New Catechism for Open Legs* and *The Compass for Cuntal Calibration* have all been inspired by penetration.

penetration is a sacred act.

Los dedos

increíble que con sólo cinco dedos en cada mano llegamos a la articulación de todas las palabras sonoras y casi todos los pensamientos.

increíble que sólo yendo de abierto a cerrado, de la boca abierta a la boca que se quiere abrir, consigamos darle sonido al sentir.

¡ah!....¡ay!....¡oooooo!........¡uuuuuuuu!....¡son tan pocos dedos y hacen tanto!

dentro de las lesbianas, las cosas pequeñas siempre se hacen grandes.

el arte lésbico es una cuestión de abrir y dejar entrar, de profundizar.

Fingers

it is incredible that with only five fingers we are able to arrive at the articulation of all the sung words and almost every thought.

incredible that with just going from open to close, from the open mouth to the mouth that wants to be opened, we can give sound to feeling.

ahhh......ohhhhh.........ooooooooooo.......uuuuuuuuuuuuu.....so few fingers and so many sounds.

within lesbians, small things are made larger.

the art of lesbianism is a question of opening and deepening.

Picotear

instrucciones:

primera: pasearse libremente por una lesbiana ya devorada. librarse de la linealidad que le impone razón al deseo. intuir las exigencias de la vagina.

segunda: detenerse en la mirada, el perfume, la temperatura, el silencio, la humedad, el momento pegajoso.

tercera: mirar qué andan haciendo los dos pezones, en qué se emplea la boca, cuál es el ritmo de la respiración, como hablan los dedos, cuál es la invitación entre los muslos.

conclusión: pasearse con el desenfado de una viajera por la piel de una lesbiana ya devorada conduce, inevitablemente, a la devoración.

Nibbling

instructions:

first: stroll leisurely over the body of a lesbian who has already been devoured. free yourself of linear thoughs that impose reason over desire. intuit the demands of a cunt.

second: linger on the look, the perfume, the temperature, the silence, the wetness, the sticky moment.

third: notice how the nipples respond, how the mouth takes shape, how the fingers flutter, how the anus contracts, how the inner thighs invite.

conclusion: strolling with the calmness of a seasoned traveller over the skin of a lesbian who has already been devoured leads, inevitably, to further feasting.

Sentir y vivir

los que piensan que se necesita "ser" para "creer" describen el camino inverso al que toman las lesbianas.

la lesbiana siente lo que es y cree suficientemente en lo que siente para serlo.

si fuera posible "ser" sin sentir, nunca llegaríamos al descubrimiento, la evocación o al vocabulario que vuela.

las que creen que primero "son" y después creen en lo que son, no toman en cuenta que uno no existe aparte de los sentimientos que acompañan al ser. "ser" sin sentir implica existir sin vivir. lo que no se siente no se vive.

solamente hay una manera de ser: sintiendo.

Feeling and Living

the ones who say that you need to "be" to believe describe the path opposite to the one that lesbians take.

the lesbian feels what she is and believes sufficiently in that she feels to "be."

if it were possible to "be" without feeling, we would never reach the discovery, or evoke the new vocabulary that is borne from "being."

the ones who think that first they "are" and later believe in what they are don't take into account that one does not exist apart from the feelings that accompany being. "being" without feeling implies existing without living. what is not felt is not lived.

there is only one way to exist: feeling

Las caras de la gente

la cara de la gente que observa a las lesbianas es otra.

las lesbianas siguen siendo las mismas; los que las contemplaron, no.

pero las lesbianas recuerdan algo de las miradas. puede ser que las escudriñaron con ojos curiosos o les clavaron la vista con violencia; de pronto las siguieron con la mirada o simplemente las vieron.

cada persona que ve una lesbiana queda marcada: la lesbiana deja la huella de su pie sobre las caras de la gente.

Other People's Faces

the face of a person who sees a lesbian changes.

lesbians continue being the same, those who contemplate lesbians do not.

lesbians are observed by curious eyes, trailed by violent beams, or simply seen.

each person who sees a lesbian is marked: lesbians leave their footprint on other people's faces.

Literatura lesbiana

los textos de las lesbianas se pasan de mano en mano y de boca en boca entre ellas mismas. se ubican sobre la piel, en la mirada, en la geografía de las palmas de las manos.

la literatura lesbiana se encuentra a pedacitos: en volantes, boletines, revistas, paredes, poemarios, notas, novelas, correspondencia electrónica, cartas de amor y desamor, pedacitos de papeles.

la literatura lesbiana también se encuentra en textos que aparentemente no tienen nada que ver con literatura ni con lesbianas: un recibo de American Express de una cena para dos en Café Aroma, los rastros de la envoltura de un preservativo rojo lubricado, el cartón de té de moras, un talonario de fósforos con "Lario's: Comida cubana en la playa" en la portada y "llámame, querida" por dentro.

las lesbianas viven en casas con escrituras en la pared que alumbran el camino hacia ellas mismas. estos textos abundan pero no se ofrecen a los demás. por eso es que parecen tan escasas las letras lesbianas—porque existen dentro de y para las lesbianas.

la literatura lesbiana es una novela con gran éxito de venta que todas las lesbiana leen todo el tiempo.

Lesbian Literature

lesbian texts are passed from hand to hand and mouth to mouth between lesbians. they are located on the skin, in the look, in the geography of the palms of the hands.

lesbian literature exists in pieces: in flyers, newsletters, magazines, chapbooks, bathroom stalls, notes, novels, e-mails, love letters, on tiny scraps of paper.

lesbian literature also exists in texts that don't seem to have anything at all to do with lesbians or literature: a customer copy of an American Express receipt, dinner for two at Café Aroma; a torn pack of Trojans that once housed bright red lubricated condoms; a box of Celestial Seasoning's raspberry zinger tea; a matchbook cover with "Lario's" on the outside and "call me soon, baby" on the inside.

lesbians live in houses with writings on the wall that indicate the way to lesbianism. these texts abound but they are offered only to lesbians; this is why lesbian literature seems scarce.

lesbian literature is the unwritten bestseller that all lesbaisn are reading, all the time: it consists of our every moment.

Para que no se me olviden las lesbianas

todas las lesbianas están hechas de mujeres que regresan a sí mismas.

las lesbianas que se nombran batallan para mantener su identidad intacta. no se contentan con existir: quieren estar ahí (en las revistas, las escuelas, los laboratorios, el cine, la literatura, las iglesias) y quieren llegar más allá (la historia, la huella, la memoria, el matriarcado).

las lesbianas insisten en documentar su lesbianismo.

así perseveran las lesbianas, repitiendo lo que son: lesbianas.

todas las lesbianas están hechas de mujeres que regresan a sí mismas.

So That I Don't Forget The Lesbians

all lesbians are made of women who return to themselves.

for self-identified lesbians, existing is not enough. they want to be present in the literature, on screen, on stage, in the body politic, in the research laboratories, in the doctrines of churches, in the icons of popular culture, in the recorded history.

lesbians insist on documenting their lesbianism.

lesbians persevere by repeating what they are: lesbians.

all lesbians are made of women who return to themselves.

Salirse de la tribu

las lesbianas forman una sociedad aparte.

aquí nos comunicamos en otro idioma, adoramos a nuestras diosas, nos inventamos nuestras propias leyes y valores.

creamos nuestra versión del paraíso: circulamos sobre valles verdes, bailamos al compás de ritmos musicales desconocidos, perfumamos el ambiente con nuestro olor salvaje.

siempre nos encontramos, siempre nos buscamos.

pero no todas podemos vivir todo el tiempo en este mundo aparte; a veces toca integrarnos a la realidad que no nos pertenece y salirnos de la tribu.

todas las lesbianas que nos salimos de la tribu encontramos la manera de seguir encontrándonos. seguimos unidas, siempre.

la tribu es tan grande como todas nosotras en todas partes, un lugar sin lugar, un hogar sin paredes, el único lugar donde pertenecemos. la tribu está hecha por cada una de nosotras.

la tribu es donde siempre nos encontramos, donde nos buscamos, donde nos unimos.

Leaving the Tribe

lesbians form a society apart.

in this society, we speak another language, worship our own deities or none at all, invent laws proper to ourselves.

we create our own version of paradise: circle upon green valleys, dance to undiscovered music, perfume the air with our wild scent.

we always find each other, always search for each other.

but not all of us can live in this world apart all of the time; sometimes we have to integrate ourselves into a society that is not ours and leave the tribe.

all lesbians who leave the tribe find a way to continue finding each other. we keep uniting, always.

the tribe is as large as all of us everywhere, a place that is not a place at all, yet our home just the same.

the tribe is each other, the only place where we belong: our sisterhood.

the tribe is where we always find each other, always search for each other: where we unite.

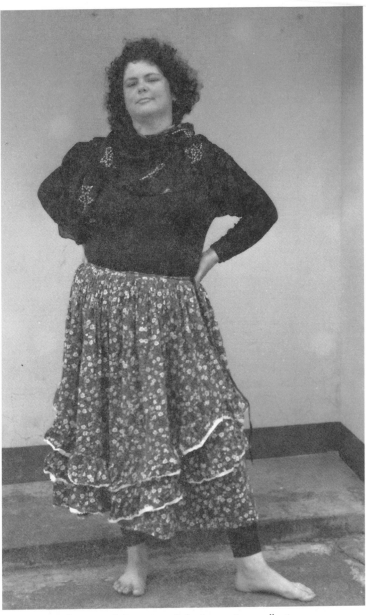

Courtesy of the tatiana de la tierra private collection.

Sobre historia fenomenológica

Para las duras: Una fenomenología lesbiana * nació en una clase. Yo estaba en mi primer semestre de una programa de creación literaria en la Universidad de Tejas en El Paso (UTEP) estudiando literatura mexicana, llenándome de escritores como Carmen Boullosa, José Emilio Pacheco, Enrique Serna, Carlos Monsiváis, y Óscar de la Borbolla. Me caían super bien estos escritores; eran ingeniosos, irreverentes e inspiradores de una manera inesperada. Pero no me gustó la tarea principal de la clase—hacer una investigación sobre la crítica literaria de una obra contemporánea mexicana.

Soy escritora, no teórica, y leo desde el punto de vista de una escritora. No me importa como otra persona pueda interpretar algo que yo lea. Las palabras me entran una por una, gota por gota. Algunas flotan dentro de mi corriente sanguínea por un rato largo, algunas desaparecen inmediatamente, incapaces de penetrarme. Yo no las controlo. Cualquier palabra—la más picante, la que forma parte de una frase lírica, la que flota como algodón, la que me acerca a mi dolor—tiene oportunidad de ser parte de mi.

Yo no quería leer artículos aburridos sobre literatura. Quería escribir en español, conducir experimentos con el lenguaje. Yo estudié en Colombia hasta el segundo grado, y decidí estudiar en El Paso precisamente para poder darme el lujo de hacer algunos de mis estudios en mi lengua materna. Le propuse a mi profesor que, en vez de hacer una investigación literaria, yo haría un experimento lingüístico creativo basado en un texto mexicano. Él requería un abstracto, entonces le entregué "Un abstracto abstracto". Él quería saber exactamente lo que yo iba a hacer, cuál texto iba a usar y cual sería mi procedimiento. Pero yo no le podía dar esos datos. Tarde o temprano llegué a un acuerdo con el profesor García: yo le entregaría mi trabajo en la última semana del semestre, y él no se iba a enterar del proyecto hasta ese preciso momento.

Yo no tenía la menor idea de qué iba a inventarme para esa clase.

La literatura mexicana que estaba leyendo era maravillosa. Me gustó la manera en que Carmen Boullosa usó una variedad de estilos en *La milagrosa*—narradores no-identificados, recortes de prensa, cartas, grabaciones, oraciones. Me acerqué instantáneamente a la narrativa de José Emilio Pacheco; leí *Las batallas en el desierto* como si se tratara de mi propia vida. Sentí envidia por la perversidad tan magnífica en *Amores de segunda mano* de Enrique Serna. Me quedé con la boca abierta con el *Nuevo catecismo para indios remisos* de Carlos Monsiváis—tan inteligente, complejo y profano. Y *Las vocales malditas* de Óscar de la Borbolla—nunca me había imaginado hasta donde se podía estirar una vocal.

Pero había un libro con tono académico que no me entraba. Más bien, lo destetaba—*Zonas de la escritura* por Dante Medina. Las *Zonas* consistían de treinta y ocho observaciones, reflexiones, teorías y ecuaciones sobre el escribir. La literatura se presentaba desde el punto de vista de un científico en un laboratorio, alguien que observa sílabas bajo un microscopio, intentando deconstruir el rastro molecular de palabras y el impacto cósmico de la puntuación. Yo no entendía ni papa. Mi nivel de español no alcanzaba las palabras magas de Medina. Leer esa doctrina densa era un reto lingüístico; me tocó usar todos mis diccionarios para entenderla. Pero cuando finalmente logré "leer" *Zonas de la escritura,* quedé fascinada. Y de alguna manera ese texto horrible se metió dentro de mi piel, en mi corriente sanguínea y en mi proceso creativo.

Comencé a lesbianizar las *Zonas* como parte de un experimento creativo. Yo estaba jugando, como suelo hacer a veces cuando me inspiro. Pensé, ¿cómo sería hablar sobre el lesbianismo de la misma manera en que Medina hable sobre la escritura? Reemplacé conceptos literarios con conceptos lésbicos y, violà—nació *Para las duras: Una fenomenología lesbiana.* Desconocía el acto de lesbianizar antes de este experimento, así que no esperaba nada en particular, pero desde el momento en que lo intenté, me pareció genial y perfecto para mi proyecto en el curso.

Fui inicialmente fiel al texto original—imité el tono estéril, copié las primeras palabras o comencé por lesbianizar el título. Por ejemplo, "La letra y el contenido, el cuerpo y el alma" resultó en "La mujer y la lesbiana: El cuerpo y el alma". El "Picotear" de las *Zonas* se trata de re-leer literatura, mientras que el "Picotear" de las *Fenomenologías* se trata de re-excitar a una mujer recién devorada. Pero mientras más lesbianizaba, más me apartaba de las *Zonas*. A fin de cuentas, lo que importa cuando uno escribe es tener una inspiración y una visión, y al darme eso, las *Zonas* ya habían cumplido con lo principal. Después de todo lo que lesbianicé, veinte y dos de las fenomenologías llegaron a esta etapa final. Me acerqué a las *Zonas* durante este proceso y llegué a apreciarlas más de lo imaginado; eran brillantes.

Escribí *Para las duras* con mucho cuidado, consultando diccionarios y correctores de pruebas con más frecuencia de lo usual. Pero me encantó hacerlo. Sentí que estaba descubriendo algo mientras que lesbianizaba. Gocé del juego y de la ciencia de mi experimento. Y logré viajar en mi mente al paraíso lésbico que llevo dentro. Recordé la primera mujer que me encantó. Estaba parada en un pasillo en el segundo piso del Departamento de Música en Miami-Dade Community College. Fumaba. Al verla me detuve en frente de ella y la miré mientras que me echaba humo mentolada en la cara. Parecía una pequeña diosa. Tenía una chispa. Llegó a ser la primera mujer que amé. Ella y todas las mujeres fantásticas de mi vida me acompañaron mientras que escribí este libro.

Para las duras: Una fenomenología lesbiana fue escrito originalmente en español e inicialmente titulado "Zonas de las lesbianas". Fue mi primer escrito significado en español; yo tenía algunos poemas y cuentos cortos en castellano, pero lo mayoría de mi prosa estaba escrita en inglés. El manuscrito original fue criticado en un taller de creación literaria de Luis Artura Ramos durante mi segundo semestre en UTEP en el departamento de español. Me fastidié por algunos de los comentarios en el taller— mis compañeros de clase criticaron la filosofía de mi "manifesto" pero no la textura y la sintaxis de la obra. Ahí fue que me di cuenta de que las *Fenomenologías* eran geniales para entrar en un plática sobre el lesbianismo.

En el otoño de 1997 fui invitada a participar en un panel de prosa en el Segundo Coloquio Internacional de Creación Literaria Femenina, un congreso auspiciado por el Departamento de Lenguas y Letras de la Universidad Autónoma de Juárez. Crucé la frontera de Estados Unidos y México para el evento y cuando llegué me sorprendí y horroricé al descubrir que Dante Medina iba a hacer una presentación. ¿Qué pensaría de lo hice con sus *Zonas*? ¿Qué tal si fuera lesbofóbico o comemierda? ¿O si me condenaba por penetrar sus ecuaciones literarias con mi puño? Lo conocí en la recepción después del congreso; el estaba elegante, vestido con una larga capa negra. Yo estaba nerviosa—jamás le había copiado el estilo a ningún escritor y necesitaba su bendición creativa. Me tragué varias copas de tequila antes de confesarle mi crimen. Se echó a reír. Se emocionó con la idea y prometí enviarle las *Zonas* lesbianizadas por correo a México. En un par de semanas recibí su aprobación en un correo electrónico.

Igual a mucho de lo que he escrito, las *Fenomenologías* se archivaron por varios años, aunque no se me olvidaron. Yo no sabía qué hacer con ellas ni dónde publicarlas. No tenía un público de lesbianas latinas con quien compartirlas. Yo estaba sola en El Paso, lejos de la tribu de mujeres que protagonizaban mi fantasía lésbica. Entonces el documento se echó a dormir en algún cajón en mi casa.

En diciembre de 1998, durante las vacaciones del invierno, me fui a Melrose, un pueblo en el norte de la Florida, y alquilé una casa de madera grande y vacía para escribir por un par de semanas. Escribí unos cuentos en español y , por primera vez, los traduje al inglés. Entonces se me ocurrió traducir las fenomenologías. Las compartí con amigas lesbianas y así tomaron vida de nuevo. (Mi traducción al inglés no es precisa, aunque hice el intento.) En 1999, durante mi último semestre en UTEP, la traducción fue criticada en un taller de creación literaria en el departamento de inglés. Yo pedí sugerencias para el título porque el de las *Zonas* me parecía aburrido. Leslie Ullman, mi profesora, me regaló la "fenomenología" del título.

"Para las duras" es otro cuento. Después de graduarme de UTEP con mi Maestría en Artes Finas, me mudé de El Paso, Tejas para Buffalo, Nueva York, donde me encerré en la universidad a estudiar bibliotecología. Mis proyectos creativos me esperaban y en el primer momento que tuve, me dediqué a resucitarlos. Saqué las fenomenologías de algún cajón y preparé el texto para publicarlo, haciendo múltiples revisiones y correcciones de prueba. Cuando lo tenía en un estado casi "perfecto", sufrí una catástrofe electrónica—el disco duro de mi computadora se reformató y perdí todo el trabajo creativo que había logrado en Buffalo. Tenía copias de mucho de mi trabajo en papel y tenía versiones electrónicas anteriores de algunas cosas, incluyendo las fenomenologías. De nuevo revisé el manuscrito y lo trabajé hacia la perfección requerida para publicación.

Pero el título no me convencía. Ya me había dado cuenta que "fenomenología" es una palabra delicada para un título—la connotación académica excita a algunas y repele a otras. A mí me encanta la academia y este libro encaja bien en cursos de estudios de mujeres y teoría queer, pero yo escribí las fenomenologías para las lesbianas—precisamente para lesbianas latinas. Por eso había modificado el título para que la "fenomenología" fuera yuxtapuesta con el ensueño de ser lesbiana. El título—*Fenomenología lesbiana: Una fantasía poética*—me parecía justo para la idea de este libro.

"Para las duras" es el resultado de amistad, buena suerte y proyectos creativos que lo consumen a uno hasta cualquier hora de la noche. Yo estaba sentada al frente de la computadora con Kim Meyerer, la artista gráfica. Ella había diseñado docenas de portadas para el libro y yo las estaba viendo por primera vez. Me fijé que Kim había puesto "para las duras" en inglés debajo del título en algunas de las portadas. Pensé que era un error; el libro está dedicado "para las duras" y ella quizás había copiado las palabras por equivocación. Pero no fue así. "Es que me gustó", dijo Kim. Estaba jugando, buscando la manera de darle algún sabor distinto a la portada. Entonces entró la novia de Kim al cuarto.

"Para las duras" dijo Garland. "Ese debería ser el título". Kim seleccionó el título y lo reemplazo con "PARA LAS DURAS". Inmediatamente me pareció preciso y brillante. Pero era casi la una de la mañana y no me sentía capaz de hacer un cambio tan radical. Además no sabía si ese título tendría tanta resonancia en español como en inglés. Me acosté pensando en las duras. "Las duras" fue un descubrimiento que me llevó a mí misma. "Las duras" me transformaron, me dieron mi propia forma y me siguen inspirando a diario. "Las duras" me prenden, me mantienen a la altera y a la espera. "Las duras" se lo merecen todo, hasta este modesto título.

No sé cómo clasificar estas fenomenologías. Las han llamado poesía, prosa, prosa poética, no-ficción creativa, una colección de aforismos, un manifiesto, una constitución lesbiana, un anhelo.

Pero no hace falta clasificarlas. *Para las duras* es serio y juguetón y utópico. Este libro explora distintos aspectos del lesbianismo, desde las uñas hasta la filosofía. Es una fantasía poética del matriarcado. No es un documento definitivo, sino un texto que continuará tomando forma. Y espero que viaje debajo de la piel, dentro de la corriente sanguínea, de las que más lo necesitan.

tatiana de la tierra
14 de septiembre de 2002, buffalo, nueva york
Escrito originalmente en inglés

*escrito 25 de noviembre de 1996, el paso, tejas, traducido al inglés 20 de diciembre de 1998, melrose, florida.

Photograph by Hilary Cellini Cook.
Courtesy of the tatiana de la tierra private collection.

On Phenomenological Herstory

*For the Hard Ones: A Lesbian Phenomenology** was conceived in a classroom. I was in my first semester of graduate school in a bilingual creative writing program at the University of Texas at El Paso (UTEP). It was the fall of 1996 and I was taking a Mexican literature class, filling myself up with the likes of Carmen Boullosa, José Emilio Pacheco, Enrique Serna, Carlos Monsiváis, and Óscar de la Borbolla. I really dug these writers; they were witty, irreverent, and inspiring in unexpected ways. But I didn't like the main assignment for the class—to research literary criticism about a piece of contemporary Mexican literature and to write an in-depth survey of these critiques.

I am a writer, not a theorist, and I read literature as a writer. I don't care about anyone else's interpretation of the words that I read. Words come into me one by one, drop by drop. Some of them float in my own bloodstream for as long as they please. Some of them are instantly eliminated from my body and mind. I don't control them, in any case. I'll give any word a chance. May the most piquant word survive, may the most lyrical phrase resonate, may the most structured plot liberate.

I didn't want to read dull texts about literature. I wanted to experiment with my own writing in Spanish—that was why I had selected UTEP for graduate school. I proposed a creative project to my professor, in lieu of a literary treatise. He wanted an abstract, which I gave him— "An Abstract Abstract." He wanted to know what exactly I would do, what text I would use, and how I would go about it. But I could not reveal such information. El profesor García finally gave me the green light; I would turn in the assignment in the last week of the semester, and he would have no idea what it would consist of until that final moment.

I also had no idea what I would come up with as a project for that class.

The Mexican literature I was reading was wonderful and completely new to me. I liked how Carmen Boullosa used a variety of writing styles in *La Milagrosa* (*The Miraculous One*), including unidentified narrators, newspaper clippings, letters, transcripts, and prayers. I became instantly cozy with José Emilio Pacheco's narration in *Las batallas en el desierto* (*The Battles in the Desert*); while reading I thought I was recalling one of my own lives. I was envious of Enrique Serna's over-the-top perversity in *Amores de segunda mano* (*Second-Hand Loves*). I was in awe of Carlos Monsiváis' intelligent, complex, and profane *Nuevo catecismo para indios remisos* (*New Catechism for Lazy Indians*). And Óscar de la Borbollas' *Las vocales malditas* (*The Wicked Vowels*)—never had I imagined how far you could stretch a vowel or the tales that a single vowel could tell.

And then there was Dante Medina's *Zonas de las escrituras* (*Zones of Writing*), my least favorite text, the one written in a scientific tone, a most alienating piece of literature. *Zonas* consisted of thirty-eight observations, ruminations, theories, and equations about writing. Writing was presented as if from the perspective of a scientist in a laboratory, one who is splicing samples of syllables, who seeks to understand the molecular traces of words and the cosmic impact of punctuation. It was heady stuff and at times difficult for me to understand; Medina is a high-end word sorcerer and my level of Spanish was not up to par. Reading *Zonas* was a linguistic and literary challenge. I employed several dictionaries as I read the dense doctrine. When I was finally able to "read" it, I became fascinated with Medina's wit. And somehow, this terrible text got under my skin, into my bloodstream, and into my creative process.

I began to lesbianize *Zonas de la escritura* as a creative writing experiment. I was just playing around. I wondered what would happen if I wrote about lesbianism the way Medina wrote about writing. I replaced literary concepts with my own lesbian concepts and violà—*For the Hard Ones: A Lesbian Phenomenology* was born. I had never heard of lesbianizing before, so I didn't expect anything in particular, but from the moment I began I thought the result was cool and perfect for my class project.

Initially, I stayed closed to Medina's text; I mimicked his sterile approach, and at times copied the first few words from the piece, or began by lesbianizing the title. For instance, "La letra y el contenido, el cuerpo y el alma" ("The Words and the Content, the Body and the Soul") eventually became "The Woman and the Lesbian: the Body and the Soul." His piece, "Picotear" ("Nibbling") is about re-reading literature, while my "Nibbling" is about re-sexing a previously-devoured woman. But the more I lesbianized, the further I went from Medina's original text. At some point, I began to use only a line or a title as inspiration. And finally, I wrote some pieces just because they wanted to be written.

Not all of the lesbianizing worked in the long run; twenty-two of them made it to this final stage. In the process, I became tight with Dante Medina's *Zonas de la escritura* and came to appreciate the text more than I ever could have imagined. It was brilliant work, after all.

I wrote *For the Hard One*s carefully, consulting more dictionaries and proofreaders than usual. It was a wonderful and gratifying process. I felt like I was making a discovery as I lesbianized. I enjoyed the game and the science of the experiment. And I was able to travel in my mind to that lesbian paradise that I carry within me. I could remember the first woman who enchanted me. She was standing outside, smoking, on the second floor of Miami-Dade Community College's Music Department. I stopped to look at her; she blew mentholated smoke in my face. She was a miniature goddess, and she had a spark. She became the first woman that I would love so. She and all the other fantastic women from my life accompanied me while I wrote this book.

For the Hard Ones was originally written in Spanish and entitled "Zonas de las Lesbianas" ("Lesbian Zones"). It was my first significant writing in Spanish, as I had mostly been writing in English. It was critiqued in Luis Arturo Ramos' fiction workshop during my second semester at UTEP. I was irked by some of the comments in the workshop—some of my fellow graduate students were more intent on critiquing the philosophy behind my lesbian "manifesto," as it was called, than on the writing's texture and syntax. On the other hand, I was able to see that the lesbianized *Zonas* proved to be a great way to talk about lesbianism within an academic setting.

In the fall of 1997, I was invited to read on the prose panel at the Second International Colloquium of Women's Creative Writing hosted by the Linguistic and Literary Studies Department of the Universidad Autónoma de Juárez. I crossed the border, from El Paso into Juárez, México for the event, and was surprised and horrified to discover that Dante Medina was a featured reader. What would he think of what I had done to his *Zonas de la escritura*? What if he was homophobic or a jerk? What if he disapproved of me for penetrating his scientifically-derived literary equations with my fist? I met him at the reception afterwards; he looked dashing in a long black cape. I was nervous. I had never used another author's work so intimately to create my own, and I needed his blessing. I swigged a shot of tequila and confessed my crime. He laughed. He seemed thrilled by the idea, and I promised to mail a copy of the manuscript to him in Mexico. Several weeks later, I got his seal of approval via e-mail.

Like many other things that I had written, *For the Hard Ones* got filed away for several years. I didn't know what to do with the phenomenologies, where to publish them. I didn't have an immediate Spanish-speaking lesbian audience for them. I was lonely in El Paso, far away from the tribe of women who were the protagonists of my fantasy.

In December of 1998, I rented a big wooden house in Melrose, Florida, during the winter break. I went there to write for a few weeks. I wrote a few stories in Spanish and then translated them into English. I had never translated anything of mine before. Then, I translated my lesbianized *Zonas* and read them to some old-time dyke friends in the area. The piece came to life again, this time in English. My translation is not exact, is not word-for-word. I was not able to render a precise translation and in some cases, I didn't want to. During my last semester at UTEP, in 1999, the English translation was discussed in a creative nonfiction workshop in the English department. I was never satisfied with the original title and sought suggestions. My professor, Leslie Ullman, gets the credit for the "lesbian phenomenology" in the title.

"For the Hard Ones" is another story. After graduating from UTEP with my MFA I moved to Buffalo, New York in the summer of 1999 to attend library school at the University of Buffalo. Again, the manuscript, along with many other creative projects, was boxed up while I became a librarian. The moment I could come up for air, I fished around for the phenomenologies; they had been put away, but I had never forgotten them. I revisited the manuscript and had it proofread over and over in preparation for publication. Once it was in a practically "perfect" state, I experienced an electronic catastrophe—my computer's hard drive was reformatted and all of my writings disappeared. I had lost all the creative work I had done in Buffalo. I did have hard copies of most things, though, and some older versions of my work, including the phenomenologies, had been saved on disk. Again, I had to revise the manuscript and have it proofread over and over until I reached the state of perfection required for publishing.

But the title was still not quite right. Based on the reactions from friends I could tell that "phenomenology" is a tricky word to have in a title—the academic connotation excites some and repels others. While I love academia and this book fits in nicely with women's studies and queer theory classes and the like, I wrote these phenomenologies for a lesbian audience—a Spanish-speaking lesbian audience, to be precise, since I did write them originally in Spanish. Thus, I modified the title so that the "phenomenology" was juxtaposed with the thrill of being a lesbian, a title that I thought covered all the bases: *Lesbian Phenomenology: A Poetic Fantasy.*

"For the Hard Ones" is a result of serendipity and friendship and late-night hours. I was looking at book covers on a computer monitor, sitting next to Kim Meyerer, the graphic artist. She had created dozens of designs for the cover and I was viewing them for the first time. I noticed that, in addition to the main title, Kim had placed "for the hard ones" on a few of the covers. This book is dedicated "for the hard ones," and I thought she had accidentally copied and pasted the first few words of the manuscript onto the cover. But it was no accident. "I just liked it," she said. She was playing around. She sprinkled it on, for flavor perhaps. Then Kim's girlfriend walked in and looked at the computer monitor.

"For the hard ones," said Garland. "That should be the title." Kim selected the title and replaced it with "FOR THE HARD ONES." Something clicked. It looked awesome and felt right-on. But it was after midnight and I wasn't convinced it would work in Spanish in the same way, so I slept on it. It continued to feel right. I realized that *For the Hard Ones* is what these phenomenologies are all about. "The hard ones" is a discovery I made that ultimately led me to myself. "The hard ones" transformed me, shaped me, and continue to inspire me. "The hard ones" is what turns me on, keeps my interest. As a title, "For the Hard Ones" is provocative, edgy, right on, and here to stay.

I don't know how to classify this work. It has been referred to as poetry, as prose, as poetic prose, as creative nonfiction, as a manifesto, as a lesbian constitution, as a collection of aphorisms, as wishful thinking. But I don't have a need to categorize it. *For the Hard Ones: A Lesbian Phenomenology* explores different aspects of lesbianism, from fingernails to philosophy. It is serious and playful and visionary. It is a poetic fantasy from the heart of the matriarchy. It is not a definite document. It is one that will continue to take shape. And, hopefully, it will journey under the skin, in the bloodstream, of those who need it most.

tatiana de la tierra
14 de septiembre de 2002, buffalo, nueva york

*written 25 de noviembre de 1996, el paso, tejas.
translated into english 20 de diciembre de 1998, melrose, florida.

Un abstracto abstracto

puede ser un milagro maldito, una zona rosa, una batalla del derecho, un viejo abecedario para niñas caprichosas, o una mujer con telaraña en el pecho. igual puede ser ninguna de estas cosas. con todos los derechos poéticos declaro: ¡por ésta selva no se mete nadie! así es que se juega al escondite con este abstracto: el resultado del proceso creativo se dará a conocer cuando la mujer araña termine de tejer.

An Abstract Abstract

it may be a damned miracle, a pink zone, a battle of rights, an outdated version of the ABCs for spoiled girls, or a woman with a spider on her chest. it could also be none of these things. with the power of my poetic rights I declare: no one enters this jungle. this is how one plays hide-and-seek with an abstract abstract. the result of the creative process will be revealed when spider woman has completed the unnamed knitting project.

Courtesy of the tatiana de la tierra private collection.

El regalo: Mi hija lesbiana
por Fabiola Restrepo,
la mamá de tatiana de la tierra

Este comentario fue publicado originalmente en 1992 en *esto no tiene nombre*. Fue compartido en *La Bloga* en Junio 2010.

El día de las madres ya pasó, pero me quedé pensando en las madres y las hijas que no lo celebraron: en la madre a quien la intolerancia selló su corazón con dolor y en la hija que sufre por el rechazo, la falta de comprensión. Y yo sé bien que mientras esa madre busca dentro de sí misma la respuesta, o no quiere aceptar la verdad, y se consume en silencio, por temor o tal vez por el qué dirán, va construyendo una muralla que la separa de su hija al final.

Yo tuve la suerte de comprender que cuando le cortaron a mi hija el cordón umbilical nos habían separado físicamente, y que lo que nos uniría después, más fuerte que un pedazo de tripa, sería el amor, el respeto mutuo, la comprensión, la aceptación. Cuando me enteré que mi hija era lesbiana, sentí confusión y dolor; pero sabía que esto era más que una palabra o un sistema de vida. Conocía la dureza de la sociedad ante este grupo de personas, la discriminación y hasta la persecución en algunos casos. Esto es algo que había yo misma pensado y sentido hacia los homosexuals toda mi vida.

Mi primer paso fue aceptar. No pensé en tratar de cambiarla ni ofrecerle llevarla al sicólogo, etc. Al fin de cuentas, bien la conozco y sé que cuando ella ha decidido un camino o encontrado una causa es porque está convencida y es para ella poseedora de la verdad.

Poco a poco, sin muchas ganas, pero con mucha curiosidad, empecé a aprender, a tratar de entender lo que hay detrás, lo que significa ser homosexual. En mi caso he visto sólo el grupo de lesbianas y quizás lo que sé de ellas es el ambiente donde mi hija se desenvuelve; ella es feminista porque abarca toda la problemática de la mujer, desde la historia, la sumisión, la subyugación, hasta la lucha por los derechos, incluso algunos en los que profundamente diferimos como es el aborto.

Ella fue parte de la editorial de *esto no tiene nombre*, revista de lesbianas Latinas (1990-1995) y sus temas fueron controvertidos. Para mí es bien atrevida al exponerlos, y algunos como el sadomasoquismo, no es que me gusten. Pero lo que sí admiro es su estilo de escribir, la forma de meterse en temas irreverentes como el poema "El día que aprendí a rezar," el poema de las mujeres con barbas, y aún más, atreverse a dejar sus pelos en la cara sin afeitar o teñir, cosa que la gente (incluyéndome a mí) no le gusta ver ni leer al respecto.

En otras palabras, entre nosotras hay diferencias, algunas muy profundas. Yo soy cristiana y ella es pagana. No acepta o reconoce a Dios y mucho menos a Jesús. Para mí el cristianismo no es sólo una creencia sino una vivencia; yo vivo mi religión. Sin embargo, para mí el amor de madre es como el amor de Dios, incondicional, y eso prevalece sobre todo. Yo estoy orgullosa de ella y todo lo que ha logrado en su vida, de lo que es como mujer y como persona. Ella tuvo el valor de dar el paso adelante cuando muchas, por el temor, se han quedado en el "closet" y por medio de la revista *esto no tiene nombre* le dió apoyo e incentivo a la comunidad.

Mi hija nació tempranito un domingo día de la madre y Dios sabía por qué me la dio en un día tan especial. Desde entonces me han obsequiado regalos finos, lindos y lujosos, pero no ha habido ninguno que la pueda igualar.

Courtesy of the tatiana de la tierra private collection.

The Gift: My Lesbian Daughter
by Fabiola Restrepo, tatiana de la tierra's mom

This was originally published in Spanish as "El regalo" in 1992 in *esto no tiene nombre*. It was later shared in *La Bloga* in June of 2010.

Mother's Day passed and left me thinking about the mothers and daughters who didn't celebrate it. I think of the mother who let intolerance close her heart in pain and of the daughter who suffers from the rejection. I know the wall this mother builds is made of silence and fear and answers that are not accepted or searched for from within. I know this wall will separate her from her daughter to the end.

When my daughter's umbilical cord was cut I was fortunate to understand that it was merely a physical separation and that what would unite us later, stronger than a band of fleshy fibers, would be love, mutual respect, understanding, and acceptance. When I found out that my daughter was a lesbian I felt confusion and pain. I knew this was more than a word or a way of life. I knew how hard society is against this group of people. I knew they were discriminated against and even persecuted at times. I knew this because these attitudes are the ones that I had felt toward homosexuals all my life.

My first step was acceptance. I didn't think of trying to change her or offering to take her to a psychologist. I know my daughter well. When she chooses a path it is because she is convinced that it possesses her truth.

Little by little, without much desire but with great curiosity, I began to learn, to try to understand what it means to be a homosexual. I've only known my daughter's lesbian world. She is a feminist who embraces woman-related issues, including history, submission, and subjugation. She even fights for women's rights, including the right to abort, which I don't agree with.

She was one of the editors of the latina lesbian magazines *esto no tiene nombre* and *conmoción* (published in Miami, 1990-1996). Her articles were controversial. She is atrevida, daring in the choice of her material. I don't like some of the things she writes about, like sadomasochism. But I admire her style of writing. And I like her way of delving into irreverent themes, as she does in the poem "The Day I Learned to Pray" and her poem about women with beards. She even lets her own facial hair grow without shaving or bleaching it, which is something that people, including me, don't like to see or read about.

In other words, we have differences between us, some of them deep. I am Christian, and she is pagan. She doesn't accept God or Jesus. For me, Christianity is more than a belief. I live my religion. For me, a mother's love is like God's love, unconditional above all. I am proud of her and everything she has accomplished in her life, of what she is as a woman and as a person. She had the courage to step forward when many, out of fear, have stayed in the closet, and through *esto no tiene nombre* and *conmoción* she supported her community.

My daughter was born on an early Sunday on Mother's Day and God knows why she was given to me on such a special day. Since then I've been given fine, luxurious gifts, but none of them have ever equaled her.

Photograph by Kim Meyerer.
Courtesy of the tatiana de la tierra private collection.

Esto no tiene nombre and *conmoción*: revistas for the hard ones
by Sara Gregory

"Words are will, what will be.
When I came out as a lesbian, words became mine more than ever—they became mirrors, herstorical documents, tools for social change. I looked for writings that reflected me, and found few. I became obsessed with creating these words that were missing. I was one of the editors of the Latina lesbian zine, *esto no tiene nombre*. Years later, I edited and published the magazine *conmoción* and the Latina lesbian writers newsletter, *el telarañazo*... I also wrote dyke columns that were printed in lesbian publications, about women's music, gay pride, going home, being in love in another country, being yourself wherever you are. I wrote love poems, erotic vignettes, pornographic stories. I wrote in English, in Spanish, in Spanglish. I wrote.
Words are what you write because you absolutely have to."
—tatiana de la tierra
A Girl with Kaleidoscope Eyes

"Without community, there is no liberation, only the most vulnerable and temporary armistice between an individual and her oppression."
—Audre Lorde
"The Master's Tools Will Never Dismantle the Master's House"

tatiana de la tierra recognized the strength of words, around them organizing networks of Latina lesbians engaged in a forum of artistic production from and beyond borders of identity, language, and cultures. *esto no tiene nombre: revistas de lesbianas latinas* and *conmoción: revista y red revolucionaria de lesbianas latinas* were zines published between 1990 and 1996 for and by Latina lesbians on a national, and eventually transnational, scale.[1] As co-founder, editor and contributor to both, tatiana's work took seriously the omission of Latina lesbians from the centers of the literary canon. Talking back to this silence, *esto* and *conmoción* demanded intersectionality, becoming spaces of access and expression for women who were often too lesbian or too Latina to be heard.

I was first introduced to tatiana de la tierra as a *Sinister Wisdom* intern. Julie was interested in acquiring the publishing rights to a de la tierra work in the hopes of reprinting it as the sixth Sapphic Classic. Reading issues of *esto* and *conmoción* (as with reading *Sinister Wisdom*), my belief in the importance of lesbian-feminist publication was again affirmed: they are sites of creativity and safety, networks of solidarity and social change, locations of intersectional critique and the un/learning of privilege and oppression. As I became more involved with the Sapphic Classic, my academic pursuits and personal passions naturally merged into my undergraduate thesis, focusing on tatiana and her work. Eventually, I even met and stayed with tatiana's mother, Fabiola, and sister Claudia, in their Miami home.

In large part, this essay is based on tatiana's own narrative of the events and people involved in publishing the zines—a narrative she admitted was not impartial. I attempt to remain faithful to tatiana's voice, using her words wherever possible not just for the sake of herstory, but because it is, after all, her story.

esto no tiene nombre

"this has no name": the way a look says desire, the way love spirals into DNA, the way dancing happens with one finger, the way

---

1 The term "revista" translated most directly to "magazine," though tatiana refers to the publications in English as "zines" I will use the terms zine and revista interchangeably, but zine culture is distinctive from that of magazines' given its DIY, non-hierarchical organization and distribution strategies, not-for-profit ethic, and counter-cultural content. The *esto* and *conmoción* collectives were volunteer-based; subscription fees covered operating costs, and discounted rates were available for poor and/or incarcerated readers.

that sisterhood travels, the way in which we walk with certainty even when there's not a word to stake a claim. ¿Qué quieres? What is your desire? esto.

Originally founded in 1990 as a newsletter and creative outlet for Miami's first Latina lesbian support and social group, Las Salamandras del Ambiente, the editorial committee of *esto no tiene nombre* included tatiana, her then-lover Margarita Castilla, and the long-time girlfriends Vanessa Cruz and Patricia Pereira-Pujol. The group would go on to publish nine issues in total of *esto*, each volume slim, controversial, and navigating "identity, desire, politics, international gatherings, building coalitions with women of color, fears, feminism, language, and being in sisterhood with each other" ("Activist Latina Lesbian Publishing Part 1").

From the start, *esto* divided Las Salamandras in two: those, like tatiana, who wanted an open, unrestricted space to publish writings, graphics, ideas, photos from as many people as possible (and who had also agreed to publish one orgasm per issue), and those who were outraged by *esto*'s erotic and political content. After a few unsuccessful mediations, Las Salamandras delivered a petition to the editorial team, calling for the revista to either disband or break from the group entirely. They broke, and though tatiana did continue to socialize with Las Salamandras on occasion, she did not forget that her own community tried to censure her voice. In her recollections, tatiana looks back on Las Salamandras as "lizard-like lesbianas who can't take the heat. They stay low to the ground and hump hidden in the shadows of shame. Salamandras are the riff-raff of the race, Christian comemierda pets of the right wing machine, pious pendejas who become skittish in the presence of potent sinvergüenzas" ("Activist Latina Lesbian Publishing Part 1").

The break did, however, expand *esto*'s vision, and left tatiana even more confident of the collective's capacity to speak beyond the needs of any one social club, or even any one city. The editorial committee needed to think bigger, to shift its focus to an international network, una telaraña de word weavers and activists. With the support of the Lambda Community Center of Greater Miami, Esto no Tiene Nombre, Inc. was officially recognized by the state of Florida (after providing an English translation for the name) in June of 1992. This change in legal status marked a significant shift in *esto*'s direction, as the group then had the ability to apply for and receive grants—something none of the women had any experience in. Moving through the grant process challenged the women to articulate their vision to an audience far removed from Miami and evaluate them in terms of money. There was a lot riding on their applications, as tatiana recalled

> wonder[ing] if foundations would understand the unique situation of lesbian immigrants who existed without the support of national organizations, centers, editorial houses or gatherings, or if they even cared. We knew we were outside of the mainstream of everything white and gay and everything heterosexual and Latino, and that venturing into these territories was inherently risky... ("Latina Lesbian Publishing Part 1").

But they knew esto was ahead of its time, and soon secured the support of various foundations including Astraea, Open Meadows Foundation, and RESIST.

The editorial team called themselves "las publicadores que hacemos todo en esto" or "the publishers who do everything in this/esto". tatiana coordinated the mailing lists and calls for submission, and regularly submitted her own poetry, Cuéntame interviews, and essays. With her talent for media, tatiana also focused on garnering a national presence by trading columns for advertising, establishing exchange subscriptions with other gay and lesbian periodicals, connecting with bookstores, and sending sample copies to women's presses—including Kitchen Table Women of Color Press, Naiad and Firebrand. Meanwhile, Vanessa wrote, typeset materials, and edited; Patricia focused on graphic art and design; Margarita kept the books, sold subscriptions, and proofread material in Spanish. Decisions were made by consensus and not always easily, but tatiana reflected

> the early days of *esto no tiene nombre* were the happiest time in my life. I had a vision, I had hope, and I was not alone. There was a lot of love going around then—sexual love, spiritual love, friendship love, literature love, publishing love. Perfect love. ("Latina Lesbian Publishing Part 2").

Gaining motion

Between 1991-1994, the nine issues Esto No Tiene Nombre Inc. published included a total 182 pages featuring 68 contributors. The zines spoke to community, to exploring the multiplicitous nature of navigating being lesbian and Latina in homophobic, racist, and classist societies. *esto* was as inclusive as possible, dedicated to "meeting people where they were at," stylistically as well as linguistically—Spanish, English, and Spanglish were all considered equally valid, and this was reflected in *esto*'s content.

By the fifth issue of *esto*, the revista was gaining traction as letters of appreciation arrived from all over el Caribe, Latin America, and Europe. Las publicadores worked to find the Latina lesbians "sprinkled throughout white lesbian enclaves in the U.S. and concentrated within Latina lesbian organizations" ("Activist Latina Lesbian Publishing Part 1). Calls-to-submissions and subscription ads were placed in *Lesbian Connection*, a long-standing newsletter founded to connect lesbians worldwide, and tatiana mobilized, calling the phone of any lesbian whose number she could find. The revista featured the works of Cherríe Moraga, Nancy Cárdenas, Juana María Rodríguez, Terri de la Peña and even tatiana's mother, Fabiola Restrepo, in "El regalo."

Despite its success, *esto* began to take its toll on las publicadoras, all of whom were financially stressed, working full time jobs, and unpaid for their responsibilities to the revista. In the summer of 1992, Hurricane Andrew, a category 5 storm, devastated the Miami area and hit the women hard.

When Hurricane Andrew ravaged South Florida on August 23, 1992, we became part of the rubble. Vane and Patri were left homeless and moved to Miami Beach. Soon after, they separated...My childhood house in Leisure City, where I still had a bedroom and many possessions, was destroyed, and my homeless family plus dog moved in with me. Margarita and I, already on shaky ground, broke up...The four of us continued to publish esto even after our relationships fell all around us, but eventually, the beauty of publishing was not stronger than the hatred we came to have toward each other ("Activist Latina Lesbian Publishing Part 1").

The collective tried to continue on with *esto,* inviting others to help with the workload, but Vanessa and Patricia soon pulled away. Amy Concepción joined as co-editor, but by then the accumulating workload, interpersonal strife, and destruction left by Andrew was too much. tatiana wanted to keep going, but *esto no tiene nombre* was over.

conmoción:

"commotion" (conmoción) and "with motion" (con moción), a powerful combination that alludes to social disturbances, earthly tremors, and all kinds of tumult. conmoción is a fury, a fervor, an endless fuck, a tempest you don't wanna tango with unless you're conmocionada, too!

From the momentum of *esto no tiene nombre,* tatiana — "la editora que echa humo", or "the editor who emits smoke" — and Amy Concepción formed *conmoción* in 1995; like *esto, conmoción* evoked allusions of their mission with a sense of humor. Surrounding this new project was a national editorial board of Latina lesbian writers, leaders, and academics, including Patricia Pereira-Pujol, Lourdes Torres, Lesley Salas, Juana Maria Rodriguez, Maria Luisa Masqué, and Terri de la Peña—all committed to expanding *conmoción*'s pull in their communities and beyond. The following garnered from *esto* springboarded the newer revista's success; the group was soon received multiple grants, signed contracts with eight distributors, and doubled the print run. Of this expansion, tatiana wrote,

Besides being larger than *esto* and involving more people in the process, *conmoción* was constructed to have direct interaction with Latina lesbian groups and also with writers. La "cadena conmoción" was focused on news about our groups and gatherings in América Latina and the US La *telaraña,* the Latina lesbian writers' web, was created as part of *conmoción.* I edited a separate newsletter, *el telarañazo* that supported emerging Latina lesbian writers. *el telarañazo* had information about where telarañeras were performing and publishing and gathering ("Activist Latina Lesbian Publishing Part 2").

Three issues of *conmoción* were published between 1995 and 1996, featuring 84 contributors from 38 cities, reaching Latina lesbianas in the U.S., Canada, Cuba, Guatemala, Chile, México, Argentina and Colombia—a readership which speaks to the momentum and necessity of their words. *La telaraña* or "spider web", website and *el telerazo* newsletter shared information about gatherings, performances, and writing opportunities in Latin America and the US

The first issue of *conmoción* explicitly dealt with activism, featuring a conversation with Cherríe Moraga, an interview between Amy Concepción and her activist self, and Carmelita Tropicana on artistic production as a weapon. Slightly longer at 48 pages, the second issue celebrates sexuality and pleasure, featuring the *cuntal* artwork of Isabell Rosado on the cover. The third issue, released in '96, explored identity. During this time, tatiana was dealing with a severe health crisis and a group of lesbians from San Francisco acted as guest editors. Meanwhile, the costs of running and producing the magazine rose as a number of distributors filed for bankruptcy and neglected their payments to *conmoción*. Shortly thereafter, *conmoción* received a series of devastating rejections from much-needed grants.

tatiana came to a critical juncture in her life. She had been diagnosed with systemic lupus in 1990 and had a serious flare up in '95. Although she loved promoting writing communities, this time around it was tatiana who needed to move on. She moved away from Miami, her family, and Margarita, who she had recently broken up with. She ended *conmoción*. tatiana went home to Colombia to heal, stating,

Colombia by then had become my haven, the place where I went to come back to life. I visited my family all over the country—from Barranquilla and Vallepudar to Bogotá and Líbano and Dorada. I went for the sheer beauty of the countryside, the volcanoes, the mountains, the ocean. I went to fall in love. And I went there to heal. Homeopathy, oxygen therapy, flower remedies, hydrotherapy—I did it all. And it was during one of those healing sessions that I decided to do something radical, to do something just for me—graduate school. I wanted to give my writing a chance and I wanted to give my life a chance, the possibility of a future ("Long and Winding Bio").

Afterlife

tatiana graduated the University of Texas at El Paso in 1999 with an MFA in Creative Writing. There, she enrolled in the bilingual literature program, wrote her thesis based on her family's story, "A Girl with Kaleidoscope Eyes," and got the inspiration for *Para las duras/For the Hard Ones*. After her graduation, tatiana continued on to the University of Buffalo and received her Master's of Library Science in 2000. There, her academic writing reflected a new interest in the politics of information and increasing accessibility of queer Latinx resources. Throughout her life, tatiana retained her passion for self-publishing, founding Chibcha Press and releasing a series of chapbooks including *The Sky That Was Only Sky* (2000), *Porcupine Love & Other Tales From My Papaya* (2005), *Píntame una mujer peligrosa* (2010), *tierra 2010: poems, songs, and a little blood* (2010) and *Pajarito, pajarito, cántame una canción* (2011). In 2009, tatiana authored the children's book *Xía y las mil sirenas*, touching on the topics of adoption and queer parenthood.

tatiana passed away on July 31st, 2012, after battling stage four cancer. She was 51 years old. Upon her death, all of tatiana's papers, unpublished works, and a complete set of *esto no tiene nombre* and *conmoción* were donated to the University of California, Los Angeles under the care of long-time friends Maylei Blackwell and Olga García Echeverría.

Now, nearly thirty years after the end of the zines, I find myself immersed in *esto no tiene nombre* and *conmoción*. I read a community of women at their most vulnerable and most bold. I am privy to the persuasiveness of their words, the depth of their injustices, the visual and poetic images of their pleasure. The topics which galvanized their contributions continue to be salient: the circulation of counter-hegemonic histories, coalition building, sex positivity, racial and ethnic inequality, nationality and belonging, survival. With recent and ongoing conversations on interlocking matrices of oppression, and a generation increasingly identifying with intersectional feminist politics, the revistas' enduring relevance (and indeed the relevance of all zines and independent publications) is only increasing. As we celebrate tatiana, my hope is that *Para las duras* continues reaching new generations of queers and creatives, infecting us with tatiana's words and passion.

Of her times with the revistas, tatiana wrote,
I think this is a story that needs to be told—we really did create history with the act of publishing. We left documents behind, we added to our body of work, and we did so, in my opinion, with a rawness and vibrancy that had not existed to date and has not been repeated since...
esto no tiene nombre and *conmoción* were tiny, unique publications, Latina lesbian megaphones. I feel fortunate to have been an integral part of their making. The early days of *esto no tiene nombre* were the happiest time in my life. I had a vision, I had hope, and I was not alone...Whenever I go to an event with Latina lesbian presence, *esto no tiene nombre* and *conmoción* are always riding on my shoulder.
Lovers and friends come and go, but magazines last forever ("Activist Latina Lesbian Publishing Part 2").

Photograph by Kim Meyerer.
Courtesy of the tatiana de la tierra private collection.

Sobre la autora: tatiana de la tierra

Nació en Villavicencio, Colombia, América del Sur el 14 de mayo de 1961.

Era dulce, tierna, obediente y amorosa.

Emigró a Mayami, Florida en 1968.

Se emputó para siempre.
Se volvió roquera y marihuanera.

Se graduó de South Dade Senior High en Homestead, Florida en 1979.

Se transformó en una hippie.

Se graduó de Miami-Dade Community College con un Associate in Arts en 1981.

Se enamoró de una mujer salvaje.
Se convirtió en una mujer salvaje.

Se graduó de la Universidad de la Florida con un Bachelor of Science en psicología en 1984.

Se convirtió en una lesbiana odia-hombres.
Se hizo masajista.
Se hizo prestamista.
Se hizo gitana.
Se hizo una femme con botas de combate.
Se hizo editora.
Se hizo activista.
Se hizo salsera.
Se hizo hedonista.
Se hizo escritora.
Se hizo pobre.

Se hizo ciudadana de los Estados Unidos de América en 1995.

Todavía estaba emputada.

Se graduó de la Universidad de Tejas de El Paso con una Master of Fine Arts en creación literaria en 1999.

Se hizo profesora.
Se hizo escritora con credenciales.
Se hizo pornógrafa.

Se graduó de la Universidad de Buffalo en Nueva York con una Master of Library Science en 2000.

Se hizo bibliotecaria.

Y la moral de este cuento es: una niña emputada se hace lo que le da la gana.

About the Author: tatiana de la tierra

Born in Villavicencio, Colombia, América del Sur, on 14 de mayo de 1961.

Was sweet and loving and content.

Emigrated to Mayami, Florida in 1968.

Became an angry girl soon thereafter.
Became a rock'n'roller and a pothead.

Graduated from South Dade Senior High, Homestead, Florida in 1979.

Became a hippie.

Graduated from Miami-Dade Community College with an Associate in Arts in 1981.

Fell in love with a wild woman.
Became a wild woman.

Graduated from the University of Florida in Gainesville with a Bachelor's in Psychology in 1984.

Became a man-hating lesbian.
Became a massage therapist.
Became a pawnbroker.
Became a gypsy.
Became a combat femme.

Became an editor.
Became an activist.
Became a salsera.
Became a hedonist.
Became a writer.
Became poor.

Became a citizen of the United States of America in 1995.

Was still pissed off.

Graduated from the University of Texas at El Paso with a Master's of Fine Arts in Creative Writing in 1999.

Became a teacher.
Became a writer with credentials.
Became a pornographer.

Graduated from University at Buffalo with a Masters in Library Science in 2000.

Became a librarian.

And the moral of the story is: One angry girl can become whatever the fuck she wants.

Sobre la artista: Maya Gonzalez

matriz maricona
fenómenos de los ríos
chicana de fuego
viaja
parada en el mismo lugar
pintando
oraciones extáticas
aperturas celestiales
enseñanzas
fantasmos
pintando
hacia arriba, hacia afuera
pintando
silencio en San Francisco.

"Oración de humo" es una pintura sobre ceremonio que aplica el sentido antiguo de humo como maestro. "Esta pintura viene de mi vida. Es una de las pocas que se parecen a mí; ese es mi tatuaje verdadero. Me recuerda que existo simultáneamente en el plano físico y espiritual. Que soy cielo y planta aprendiendo a liberarme a través del fuego. Es una pintura de poder que me hace consciente de quién yo soy y qué hago aquí."

— Maya Gonzalez
www.mayagonzalez.com

About the Artist: Maya Gonzalez

queer
river femme freak
fire Chicana
travels
standing in the same spot
painting
elastic prayer
sky opening
lessons
haunts
painting
up and out
painting
San Francisco silence.

"Smoking Prayer" is a painting about ritual that uses the ancient meaning of smoke as teacher. "It was drawn from my life and is one of the only pieces I've ever done that looks like me—that is my real tattoo. It reminds me that I am physical and spiritual at the same time. That I am sky and plant learning to be free through fire. It is a power piece, reminding me of who I am and what I'm doing here."

— Maya Gonzalez
www.mayagonzalez.com

Mil gracias

A mis correctores de pruebas y asesores literarios: Martha Treviño, Beatriz Arellano, Margarita Castilla, Roberto Tejada, Luis Aguilar-Moreno, Lorna Perez, Flora Maria Uribe, Jaime Riascos, Hector García, Roberto López, Olga García y mis compañeras de estudio en la clase de creación literaria en los departamentos de inglés y español en at UTEP.

A amig@s que contribuyeron opiniones valiosas el título, el texto y el diseño durante el tiempo en que se maquinaba este libro: Juana Maria Rodriguez, Ernesto Martínez, M. Renee Prieto, Carmen Corrales, Alex Flores, Alma Lopez, Masani Alex de Veaux, Aprille Nace, Marcia Ochoa y l@s escritores berrac@s del Salón de Belleza.

A mis profesores en UTEP: Fernando García Nuñez, Luis Arturo Ramos y Leslie Ullman.

A Dante Medina, autor de *Zonas de la escritura* (*Zones of Writing*, Jalisco, México: Universidad de Guadalajara, 1994), por la inspiración.

A Albalucía Ángel, autora de *Las andariegas* (*The Wanderers*, Barcelona: Editorial Argos Vergara, 1983), por el encantado.

A Maya Gonzalez por el arte.

A Kim Meyerer por las gráficas.

A Garland Godinho y Kim Meyerer, por "para las duras".

A Patricia Pereira-Pujol, por la edición.

A Judith Hopkins, por ayudarme a catalogar.

133

A los mejores bibliotecari@s de todo el mundo en la Biblioteca de Undergraduates en la Universidad en Buffalo, por la solidaridad.

A Andres Tangarife y Gloria Eugenia Tangarife, por ser mi familia.

A mi mamá, Fabiola Restrepo, por siempre dejarme ser la persona que soy.

A mi hermano, Gustavo Alberto Barona, por el apoyo económico que me permitió ser una lesbiana internacional y por siempre ser tan chévere.

A Manu, el hombre eléctrico, por la ciber-fantasía.

A todas las mujeres que me amaron y me aguantaron todos estos años, por lo que no se nombra.

A los Chibchas, a mis antepasad@s, a mis abuelitas y a Colombia, por la fortuna.

A Margarita Castilla, por la musa.

A El Salón de Belleza, por la alegría.

A Ochún, por el placer.

Very Special Thanks

To my proofreaders and literary advisors: Martha Treviño, Beatriz Arellano, Margarita Castilla, Roberto Tejada, Luis Aguilar-Moreno, Lorna Perez, Hector García, Flora Maria Uribe, Jaime Riascos, Roberto López, Olga García, and fellow graduate students in creativing writing workshops from the Spanish and English departments at University of Texas at El Paso.

To friends who contributed valuable opinions about titles, text, and design during the making of this book: Juana Maria Rodriguez, Ernesto Martínez, M. Renee Prieto, Carmen Corrales, Alex Flores, Alma Lopez, Masani Alex de Veaux, Aprille Nace, Marcia Ochoa, and the bad-ass writers from The Beauty Salon.

To my professors at UTEP: Fernando García Nuñez, Luis Arturo Ramos, and Leslie Ullman.

To Dante Medina, author of *Zonas de la escritura* (*Zones of Writing*, Jalisco, México: Universidad de Guadalajara, 1994), for the inspiration.

To Albalucía Ángel, author of *Las andariegas* (*The Wanderers*, Barcelona: Editorial Argos Vergara, 1983), for the enchantment.

To Maya Gonzalez for the artwork.

To Kim Meyerer for the graphics.

To Garland Godinho and Kim Meyerer, for "for the hard ones."

To Patricia Pereira-Pujol, for the editing.

To Judith Hopkins, for assistance with cataloguing.

To the best librarians in the world at University at Buffalo's Undergraduate Library, for the solidarity.

To Andres Tangarife and Gloria Tangarife, for being my family.

To my mom, Fabiola Restrepo, for giving me permission to be myself.

To my brother, Gustavo Alberto Barona, for sponsoring my international lesbian activities when I was broke and for always being the coolest bro.

To Manu, the electrician man, for the cyber fantasy.

To all the women who loved me and put up with me all of these years, for that which has no name.

To the Chibchas, to my ancestors, to my grandmothers, and to Colombia, for the fortune.

To Margarita Castilla, for the muse.

To the Beauty Salon, for the joy.

To Ochún, for the pleasure.

Selected Bibliography

Books:

Para Las Duras: Una Fenomenologia Lesbiana / For the Hard Ones: A Lesbian Phenomenology. San Diego, CA: Calaca, 2002.
Píntame Una Mujer Peligrosa. Buffalo, NY: Chibcha, 2005.
Porcupine Love and Other Tales from My Papaya. Buffalo, NY: Chibcha, 2005.

Articles

"Activist Latina Lesbian Publishing: Esto No Tiene Nombre and Conmoción." *Aztlan: A Journal of Chicano Studies*, 27.1 (2002): 139-78.
"Aliens and Others in Search of the Tribe in Academe." *This Bridge We Call Home Radical Visions for Transformation*. Ed. c and AnaLouise Keating. New York: Routledge, 2002.
"Compañeras : Latina Lesbians : An Anthology." *Compañeras: Latina Lesbians: An Anthology*. By Juanita Ramos. New York: Routledge, 1994.
"Dancing with Daisy." *Gynomite: Fearless Feminist Porn*. Ed. Liz Belile. New Orleans: New Mouth from the Dirty South, 2000. 30-35.
"The Fire in My Heart." *This Bridge We Call Home Radical Visions for Transformation*. Ed. Gloria Anzaldúa and AnaLouise Keating. Florence: Taylor and Francis, 2013.
"In Gay Code: Everything We Should Know." *School Library Journal* 48.4 (2002): S51.
"Latin American Lesbian-Feminists Together in Mexico." *Visibilities* Sep./Oct. 1988: 8-11.
"Latina Lesbian Literature." *Encyclopedia of Hispanic-American Literature*. Ed. Luz Elena. Ramirez. New York, NY: Facts On File, 2008. 192-94.

"A Lesbian Journey Through the Fog." *Viva Arts Quarterly* 1995: 15-16.

"Neurotic Love Letters." *Journal of Lesbian Studies* 8.3 (2004): 93-96.

"Queer books bloom in Spain." *Curve*, June 2004, p. 52+.

"Argentina: Lesbian Visibility." *Ms Magazine*, vol. 1, no. 6, 05 1991, pp. 16.

"Barriers to Selecting Materials about Sexual and Gender Diversity." *Serving LGBTIQ Library and Archives Users: Essays on Outreach, Service, Collections and Access.* Jefferson, NC: McFarland, 2011.

"Coming Out and Creating Queer Awareness in the Classroom: An Approach from the U.S.-Mexican Border." *Lesbian and Gay Studies and the Teaching of English: Positions, Pedagogies, and Cultural Politics.* Ed. William J. Spurlin. Urbana: National Council of Teachers of English, 2000. 163.

"Jail Time for Beginners." *Latino Heretics.* Ed. Tony Diaz. Normal, IL: Published by Fiction Collective Two, 1999. 67.

"A Latina Lesbian Activists's Survival Guide, O Mejor Dicho, Activism De-mystified, De-glorified & De-graded." *Latino Heretics.* Ed. Tony Diaz. Normal, IL: Published by Fiction Collective Two, 1999. 64-67.

"Prisoner of Hope: Gustavo Álvarez Gardeazábal." *El Andar* 12.1 Spring 2001: 50-53.

"Silencing Our Lady : La Respuesta De Alma." I Am Aztlán: The Personal Essay in Chicano Studies. Ed. Chon A. Noriega and Wendy Laura. Belcher. Los Angeles, CA: UCLA Chicano Studies Research Center, 2008.

"Swine-juvenile Literature?: Good Cataloging vs. Good Public Service." *Radical Cataloging: Essays at the Front.* By K. R. Roberto and Sanford Berman. Jefferson (North Carolina): McFarland, 2008.

"Juego." *The Second Coming.* Ed. Pat Califia and Robin Sweeney. Los Angeles: Alyson, 1996. 224.

Archives:

tatiana de la tierra's writing, #7710. Division of Rare and Manuscript Collections, Cornell University Library.

tatiana de la tierra Latina lesbian magazine collection, CEMA 167. Department of Special Collections, UC Santa Barbara Library, University of California, Santa Barbara.

Tatiana de la Tierra Papers, 124, UCLA Chicano Studies Research Center, University of California, Los Angeles.

Compiled by Sara Gregory (March 2017).

Para que no se me olviden las lesbianas.

So that I don't forget the lesbians.